STUDIES IN MODERN EUROPEAN
LITERATURE AND THOUGHT

General Editors:

ERICH HELLER

*Professor of German
at Northwestern University*

and

ANTHONY THORLBY

*Lecturer in German
in the University College of Swansea*

BENJAMIN CONSTANT

BENJAMIN CONSTANT

BY

WILLIAM W. HOLDHEIM

*Associate Professor of European
Languages and Literature
Brandeis University*

NEW YORK
HILLARY HOUSE PUBLISHERS LTD
1961

*Printed in Great Britain
by Richard Clay and Company Ltd,
Bungay, Suffolk*

TO EVA

CONTENTS

ACKNOWLEDGMENT

I wish to thank all the friends who generously helped me when I was writing this monograph. I notably mention Professor Lewis A. Coser of Brandeis University, who gave valuable advice on the political chapter, Professor Thalia Ph. Howe of Brandeis University, who greatly helped me with the stylistic revision of certain parts, Professor Hans Meyerhoff of the University of California at Los Angeles, who gave me advice and encouragement in the early stages of the writing, and especially Professor Eléonore M. Zimmermann of Brandeis University, who read the entire manuscript and made many helpful suggestions about both style and contents. Thanks are also due to Brandeis University for financial assistance in the typing of the manuscript.

WILLIAM W. HOLDHEIM

Waltham, Mass.,
May 30, 1960

BENJAMIN CONSTANT

I

CONSTANT'S PERSONAL LIFE

The story of Constant's life has tempted many biographers and struck the imagination of all readers. Born in 1767 in Lausanne, a descendant of French Protestants who had left France for religious reasons, Benjamin Henri Constant de Rebecque lived at a crucial period in history. He survived the last years of the Ancien Régime, the French Revolution, the Napoleonic era, and played an outstanding role in the France of the Restoration. Thus he was a lucid witness, and more, of the events which accompanied the transition from the eighteenth to the nineteenth century and gave birth to our modern world. More than that: his personal life was as eventful and troubled as contemporary European history.

Constant lost his mother very early, and his father, Louis Arnold Juste Constant—a colonel in the Swiss regiment of the Dutch army—was an unstable, timid, violent man and hardly an ideal educator. His pedagogy may be described as an experiment in perpetual uprooting, ranging from Switzerland to Brussels and Bois-le-Duc, and was complicated by a succession of grotesque private tutors usually debauched, ignorant, or weak, and often all at the same time. Their authority was hardly enhanced by Juste's unfortunate propensity for disliking them and imparting his ironic contempt to the child. But Benjamin's intellectual development did not suffer. At the age of five he was learning Greek and at seven spending eight to ten hours a day devouring fashionable novels and irreligious treatises. His childhood letters show striking precocity and already contain the later Constant in miniature.

Juste did his best to encourage this intellectual precocity and in 1780 tried to place his thirteen-year-old son in Oxford University, which of course could not admit him because of his age. At fifteen, however, Benjamin was admitted to the University of Erlangen in the small German principality of Anspach, where he studied diligently while expressing the most absurd views on everything, ridiculing everybody, and running up gambling debts. But thanks to his father's friendship with the Margrave he was well received at the Court until, out of sheer bravado, he began to appear in the company of a young lady of doubtful reputation whose family had offended the Dowager. Constant, in disgrace, had to leave.

His next sojourn was at the University of Edinburgh, which then was famous for its intellectual atmosphere and where he met men like Adam Ferguson. With ample opportunity to indulge his passion for learning, Constant concentrated upon ancient history and literature and, as a result, published an anonymous translation of Gillies' *History of Greece*. Yet, though he later described his eighteen months in Edinburgh as the most pleasant period of his life, he left in somewhat obscure circumstances, probably connected with gambling debts. By 1785 young Constant, who had become remarkably learned and already fluent in both English and German, was in Paris for the first time. Only a few months later, however, Juste had to come and rescue his son from the temptations of the capital. But within two years, after a stay in Brussels and Switzerland, Benjamin was back in Paris. During his Brussels stay he had his first real love affair— with Madame Johannot, an unhappily-married Genevese lady who, like many of his later mistresses, was considerably older than he.

The Paris of 1787 was in that particularly agreeable and stimulating state of intellectual ferment which often characterizes the last years of a declining era. At the home of his host, the writer and publicist Suard, Constant met such eminent men as Condorcet, d'Alembert, Garat, and La Harpe. He became an habitué of several leading salons, listened to lectures on philosophy and literature at the "Lycée", a fashionable academy, and at the same time led his customary dissolute life.

His outstanding experience of that period, however, was his friendship with Isabella van Serooskerken van Tuyll, twenty-seven years his senior. "Belle" van Tuyll, of an aristocratic Dutch family, was an extraordinary woman, who had married her brothers' Swiss tutor, a Monsieur de Charrière, a devoted husband but a mediocre man. All of Belle's former suitors, James Boswell among them, had recoiled before this woman's brilliant intellect and masculine aggressiveness. A writer of pre-romantic novels of some note, she lived for the most part near Neuchâtel, where she was isolated from society, since her books were full of mockery for social conventions; the alert and critical mind of this child of the eighteenth century accepted no sham and no pretence. For twelve years Belle van Tuyll had corresponded with Benjamin's uncle, David de Constant, a friend of Voltaire, and in her letters showed a disconcerting frankness and the most lucid self-perception. Such qualities appealed to Benjamin, for they encouraged his own propensities. Though it is not known whether he ever became the lover of Madame de Charrière, the two spent whole nights in brilliant and untiring conversation, ridiculing established values and Benjamin's follies.

Constant supplied them with ample cause. His father had wanted him to marry Jenny Pourrat, a wealthy girl, and when Benjamin failed, Juste sent an officer to bring him to Bois-le-Duc. Instead, Benjamin fled to England, where he roamed adventurously about, borrowing money and visiting friends as far distant as Edinburgh. His letters to Madame de Charrière describe this gay and utterly irresponsible period of his life. After a few months, lacking funds, the adventurer was forced to return to his father, who now obtained for him the position of underchamberlain to the Duke of Brunswick. In 1788 Constant arrived at that Court, where he was to remain for several years.

It was a most unhappy period in his life. Constant found the Court ceremoniously dull, the people ponderous, while his frequent tactlessness estranged him from other courtiers. Soon his sympathies for the revolutionists in France made him feel even more alienated, so that partly from loneliness, partly from pity he married a lady-in-waiting to the Duchess, Minna von Cramm, a plain woman who was as lonely as he. The marriage was unhappy from the beginning: there was neither love nor mutual understanding. Minna acquired a number of lovers and treated her husband with contempt, and they divorced as soon as possible. During the same period, so wretched for Benjamin, his beloved father succeeded in losing a series of lawsuits and, in addition, through an imprudent act exposed himself to disciplinary measures in the army. Benjamin defended his father with almost fanatical loyalty, but Juste was ruined and his position lost. All these misfortunes cast Benjamin into a profound despair, a pessimism more than temporary. "I have learnt too clearly that in standing aside and seeing nothing but the absurdity of things one touches no depths," he wrote to his aunt, Madame de Nassau. ". . . I am tired of my own mockery, I am tired of surrounding my heart with a mist of dismal indifference that shuts me out from every experience of happiness."[1] No longer able to bear the emotional aridity of his ironic detachment, he craved real feeling, "the folly of enthusiasm".

This boded ill for his friendship with the cynical Madame de Charrière. Constant had remained in regular correspondence with her and more than once had visited her in Switzerland.

[1] Quoted this way in Geoffrey Scott, *The Portrait of Zélide* (London, 1931), p. 166.

Though his marriage with Minna had scarcely weakened her influence over Constant, Madame de Charrière swiftly sensed danger when in 1794 Constant, who by then had permanently left Brunswick and had returned to Switzerland, met Madame de Staël.

In the eyes of the aristocratic Madame de Charrière, Necker's daughter ("the too famous one", as she called her) was a vulgar theatrical parvenue. A Belle van Tuyll could not condone Madame de Staël's pretentiousness, her gushing exhibitionism, the sentimentality and rhetoric which were rarely absent from her writings. But her friend, who had so often joined her in mocking these faults, upon meeting Madame de Staël was conquered by her conversational brilliance and even more by her warmth and "enthusiasm", the very qualities he sought and needed to give meaning to his life. To Constant, Madame de Staël seemed to represent a new and infinitely more vital age. He courted her with little success at first, but his perseverance won, and Madame de Charrière wryly acknowledged defeat. Constant and Madame de Staël signed a pledge to devote their entire lives exclusively to each other, and thus there began her fatal reign of seventeen years.

In 1795, shortly after the fall of Robespierre, Constant went with Madame de Staël to Paris, where the tall, red-haired, lanky young man, who had been notorious for his sartorial negligence, suddenly turned into a *muscadin*, a typical dandy of the Directoire period who moved with ease and relish in Parisian society. Under the aegis of his distinguished companion, he was initiated into politics, and he promptly turned his energies to the pursuit of these new ambitions. (But this important aspect of Constant's activity will be discussed in Chapter IV.) Meanwhile the mutual pledge of eternal love proved rather short-lived, for soon after her arrival in Paris Madame de Staël formed a violent attachment for another, François de Pange. Constant on his part wrote to his aunt as early as 1796, asking her to look for a girl he might marry, but retracted his request a few weeks later: Madame de Staël's daughter Albertine was born, and it is likely that Constant was the father.

The year 1800 brought a new liaison, between Constant and Anna Lindsay, a beautiful and sensitive woman of Irish origin, who, quite unlike Madame de Staël, was deeply feminine. A courtesan in the grand style, Chateaubriand called her "the last of the Ninons". Her correspondence with Constant is justly famous: like an intense, dramatic novel, it reveals Constant, at first swept away by passion, gradually becoming reasonable, detached, and evasive. At the same time there is

Anna's growing love, the sinuous torment of her gnawing doubts and her jealousy. It was she who finally ended the relationship because of Constant's refusal to break with Madame de Staël, who due to political reasons was by then a *persona non grata* in Paris. In later years Constant's liaison with Anna was renewed several times, and he realized that no other woman had ever loved him so completely and unreservedly: "To her I owe having known all the fever of physical and mental love in a woman."[2]

Another close friend of Constant, though not his mistress, was Julie Talma, the estranged wife of the great actor. She was a genuine disciple of the last eighteenth-century *philosophes* and her home was one of the chief political and literary salons of that period. Constant admired her for her clarity of mind and judgment as well as for her strength and generosity, and few events in his life affected him as deeply as Julie Talma's death in 1805.

Constant was hostile to Napoleon and spent the major part of the Napoleonic era outside of France, although he was not forced into exile, like Madame de Staël. During the first decade of the new century his relationship with Madame de

[2] Journal of 28 July 1804. All Constant quotations have been translated by myself, except where otherwise indicated.

Staël degenerated into an endless drama of mutual torment. Her possessiveness was enormous; and although she had other lovers, she succeeded in holding Constant captive in her sphere. "There is in her a combination of violence and affection which shakes the very core of my soul," he wrote in one letter, "and I feel that I can neither live in the continual anguish in which her reproaches, complaints, explosions, and dejection always keep me, nor bear to break a bond she is determined to maintain at all costs."[3] His journal of those years records the perpetual fluctuations of their struggle, the terrible scenes followed by excruciating reconciliations. It reveals Constant's eternal vacillations, his complete dependence on changing moods. Intellectually and emotionally blocked by Madame de Staël's egocentricity, he often hated her, only to love and admire anew her vitality and generosity. Moreover, he was trapped by his almost morbid fear of causing anyone pain, an admirable trait that was balanced by one less admirable: his fear of the harm she might do him in public opinion if he left her.

In 1804 Constant accompanied Madame de Staël to Germany, a journey that became crucial

[3] Letter of 20 July 1807 to his cousin, Rosalie de Constant. In *Benjamin et Rosalie de Constant: Correspondance. 1786–1830* (Paris, 1955), p. 62.

in his intellectual development. His extensive reading of German works of philosophy, literature, and scholarship made him an expert on German contemporary intellectual tendencies. At the libraries of Leipzig and Göttingen he continued research on comparative religion, a study begun in 1785 and which occupied him for the rest of his life. In Weimar, Constant met the great men of contemporary German literature: Schiller, Wieland, and Goethe. Schiller he liked, attracted by his ideas and his personality, but his reaction to Goethe was more complex. Though impressed by Goethe's depth and intelligence, Constant never felt entirely at ease with him. Above all, he objected to the streak of aesthetic amoralism in Goethe's character: it struck him as an essential lack of *goodness*. If we judge from his diaries, Constant did not fully appreciate Goethe's literary qualities. His criticism of *Iphigenie*, although too harsh, is at least intelligent. But his comparison of *Faust* (albeit the early version) with Voltaire's *Candide*, to the advantage of the latter, is by far the worst literary judgment he ever pronounced.[4]

Constant's happiness with Madame de Staël improved during that time. He returned to Switzerland, while she proceeded to Berlin alone. On learning, however, of her father's sudden

[4] Cf. Journal of 12 February and 12 March 1804.

death, he hurried back to her and broke the sad news. But by the summer of 1805 he was in attendance again at Coppet, the Necker family castle, where his bondage weighed on him as heavily as ever. This was the greatest period of Madame de Staël's career, when her fame could almost vie with that of her enemy, Napoleon. Coppet became a meeting-place for many distinguished men, a centre for German-French intellectual exchange. Its chatelaine was surrounded by a brilliant court, including Bonstetten, Sismondi, and August Wilhelm Schlegel. Many such visited Coppet, among them Byron, Chamisso, Zacharias Werner, and Friedrich Schlegel. It is interesting to read Constant's reaction to the brothers Schlegel. He disliked Friedrich and, strangely enough, was rather jealous of August Wilhelm, who exerted considerable influence on Madame de Staël. Constant admired August Wilhelm's erudition, but remarked that his judgments often lacked taste while his ideas tended to be grotesque and monotonous. In general, he had little sympathy for the romantic philosophy of the Schlegels and was wary of its reactionary catholicizing tendencies.

More than once in this period Constant had thought of marrying Madame de Staël, whose estranged husband, the former Swedish ambassador to Paris, had died in 1802. Nothing had come of this plan, as with so many others: Constant was fundamentally unenthusiastic, his pleas were unconvincing, and, furthermore, Madame de Staël did not wish to compromise her independence. At other times he believed that he could escape from her yoke only by marrying another woman, and looked upon such a marriage as a haven of peaceful refuge. Consequently, he was always in search of a suitable partner, but could never bring himself to take a decisive step. Finally in 1805, during a stay in Paris, he met, once again, Charlotte Dutertre, formerly Charlotte von Hardenberg.

Constant had known Charlotte in Brunswick in 1793, when he was in process of divorcing Minna von Cramm and at a time when Charlotte was also on the point of separating from her first husband, the Baron von Marenholz. The two became virtually engaged, but Constant's indecision and the opposition of Charlotte's father prevented their marriage. They drifted apart, their correspondence gradually ceased, and in 1798 Charlotte married Monsieur Dutertre. As soon as they met again, it became evident that Charlotte was still in love with Constant. Not long afterwards he became her lover, and for him she obtained a divorce once more. But their story during the following years is perhaps without parallel in the annals of human weakness. Torn between two shaky loyalties—between his inability to resist, on the one hand, Madame de Staël's will and, on the other, a love subjected to endless vacillation—Constant drifted aimlessly along, always taking the road of least resistance. He spent much of his time in Coppet, where his presence was imperiously demanded. Again and again he put off any decision, dreaming in the meantime of the "angelic" Charlotte, who suffered because of him. It was Charlotte's feminine gentleness and humility which appealed to him, partly because it contrasted with Madame de Staël's lack of them. The latter, consumed by jealousy, became increasingly violent, so that an entry in Constant's diary for 1807 describes her as "fury" and a "scourge". "Always her suffering as a means and her nature as a motive," he notes on May 27. "My God, deliver us from each other." The climax came on September 1st: Constant fled on horseback from Coppet, and Madame de Staël followed and overtook him, forcing his return by pleas, screams, and hysteria. He now renounced all thought of further revolt and sought consolation in religion, until in June 1808, taking advantage of the virago's absence, he secretly married Charlotte in Besançon. Only a year later, Madame de Staël found out, but through Charlotte herself—Constant had not dared tell her! Madame de Staël haughtily demanded that he continue to keep his marriage a secret. After numerous other vicissitudes, including a suicide attempt by Charlotte, the final separation with his tyrant came in 1811. By then Madame de Staël herself had been secretly married for some time.

Constant at a later period pointedly did justice to Madame de Staël's many good qualities: her spontaneity, her loyalty to her friends, her pity for the persecuted. The truth is, her former lover sometimes regretted that he had broken with her. Meanwhile his relations with Charlotte, who could not compete with the brilliant intellect of her predecessor, deteriorated very soon, though she remained his wife to the end.

Constant spent the years from 1811 to 1813 in Germany, mostly in Göttingen, continuing his work on comparative religion. Finally, after the fall of Napoleon, he returned to France, where for the last seventeen years of his life he devoted himself chiefly to politics. But it was at this point, soon after his return, that Constant met with the last great passion of his life.

The beauty of Juliette Récamier has become proverbial. Among her numerous admirers she counted some of the most distinguished figures of the early nineteenth century. Constant, who had known her for a long time without showing particular interest, suddenly was overwhelmed by her charms. Perhaps his infatuation was merely an ageing man's desperate longing for emotion. But his love was unrequited, and Madame Récamier made him suffer more than any other woman he had known. His journal of 1814–15 records the anguish of his useless efforts to gain her affection and his endless alternation between hope and despair. Yet at the same time the diary reveals his capacity for cruel and penetrating observation. His ability to detach himself from his own emotions was one of Constant's most striking characteristics: "I am not a completely real being," he once wrote about himself. "There are two persons in me, one observing the other, well knowing that his convulsive movements will pass."[5] Even in the midst of his passion for Madame Récamier, her admirer clearly saw in her the basic superficiality of the coquette, thereby measuring the extent of his folly. His "récit de Juliette", which dates from that time, is a small masterpiece of psychological penetration. It is purportedly an account of Adrien de Montmorency's courtship of Juliette, as told in her own words, but its terrible irony bears the imprint of Constant. The fragment reveals a woman avid for public applause and deceived into regarding her emotional frigidity as the triumph of will over desire.

[5] Journal of 11 April 1804.

The "récit de Juliette" was destined to be part of Constant's *Mémoires*, which he had begun to write at the suggestion of Madame Récamier. These memoirs, which have remained fragmentary, are by no means Constant's only attempt at autobiography: his chief literary works are in large part based upon his life.

II

AUTOBIOGRAPHY AS LITERATURE

The artistic merit of Benjamin Constant's works has always been recognized, and his novel *Adolphe* is one of the classics of French literary history. Nevertheless, there has been a traditional over-emphasis on the purely biographical aspect of his writings, often at the expense of their artistic appreciation. *Adolphe*, the *Cahier rouge*, and more recently *Cécile* have been used rather indiscriminately to throw light on the author's life and personality—always a dangerous procedure. Conversely, too much weight has been given to the events of his life in *explaining* the creation of his works. This tendency was strengthened by an implicit, often unverbalized assumption which is perhaps unique in the history of criticism. To put it bluntly, there was, and still is, a widespread belief that Constant was not really a *creative novelist*. A frequently cited passage from his journals, which is now known to be apocryphal, states that he wrote *Adolphe* in two weeks, merely to win a bet. Other remarks, mostly dating from a period in his life when he was completely engrossed in political activity, seem to suggest that he attached little importance to his literary efforts. Thus there arose the image of the gifted dilettante who wrote partly for his pleasure, partly for the purpose of clarifying the processes of his own mind, and whose introspective lucidity enabled him to seize and elucidate the secret structure of his experiences so that, as by a miracle, they took on literary form.

We must reject an interpretation which in effect equates literary form with psychological structure, denies the creative process by affirming its coincidence with self-observation, and thus establishes a too simple relationship between life and art. An author's professed opinions are often a poor criterion for judging his work. Besides, at other times Constant made no secret of his literary ambitions. It is true that as far as we know, his more important literary works were all written within a limited span of years, during the troubled period from 1806 to 1811. Yet he was a *genuine* novelist, eminently versed in the art of aesthetic elaboration. His writings, valuable as they are for a knowledge of the man, cannot be identified with his life, and the critic should insist on their primarily *literary* character. But Constant's repeated experiments with autobiography do reveal some of the problems inherent in this genre and clarify the relationship between literature and life, the complexity of which cannot be grasped by a "biographical" approach.

The Cahier rouge

Constant's uncompleted autobiography, *Ma vie*, more generally known as the *Cahier rouge*, was written in 1811, but remained unpublished until 1907. This brief account retraces the first twenty years of the author's life, his turbulent cosmopolitan childhood and adolescence, ending in 1787, not long after his English escapade. Constant tells about his youthful follies without complacency or self-indulgence, with an inimitable irony not entirely free from sadness. Of course there can be no question of noting everything, since the very process of narration naturally imposes a choice. But even beyond such necessary omissions this autobiography is strongly and deliberately stylized.

Three amusing episodes will serve to characterize the general tone and atmosphere of the story: the adventure with Mrs Trevor, the courting of Mademoiselle Pourrat, and the misunderstanding with Madame Saurin. In Lausanne in 1786 Mrs Trevor, a somewhat mature English lady separated from her husband, offered

"friendship" in return for young Benjamin's pro-
testations of love. This obvious synonym became an insurmountable barrier and reduced the
youth to a state of foaming despair which could
not be alleviated by the lady's obvious readiness
to console him by all the means at her disposal.
Later in Paris Benjamin courted Jenny Pourrat at
his father's desire. In passionate letters he
promised to rescue her from her parents' tyranny,
ignoring the fact that she was not in love with
him and that the parents, far from tyrannical,
looked upon his courtship with some favour. At
the same time, he never so much as referred to
love when he was alone with his "beloved". He
finally ended the whole affair through a fake
attempt at suicide in her house, and at a moment
when everybody was frantically trying to save his
life he was overcome by irresistible boredom and
detached himself from the feverish excitement he
had caused. The third incident is still more
grotesque, if possible. Madame Saurin "had been
very beautiful and was the only one to remember
it, for she was sixty-five".[1] Benjamin, in debt as
usual, wrote her a letter asking for a loan and
then paid her a visit, only to discover on his

[1] In Benjamin Constant, *Oeuvres*, Pléiade edition (Paris,
1957), p. 133. All page references will be to this edition,
except where otherwise indicated. This edition has also
been used for Constant's *Journaux intimes*.

arrival that Madame Saurin had not received his note. In his consternation he presented his request in such a confused manner that the elderly lady took it for a declaration of love and reacted with palpitating and all-too-promising excitement. "This error," Constant writes, "her emotion, and the proximity of a large red damask bed threw me into inexpressible terror."[2] The misunderstanding was cleared up in panic haste, the loan was granted, and they parted in speechless embarrassment.

Misunderstanding caused by overpowering timidity is the common characteristic of these delightful adolescent adventures. An even more extreme episode of this kind is the description of the famous meeting between Constant and his father in Bois-le-Duc, near the end of the book. Benjamin returns from his illicit English escapade, trembling in expectation of the paternal ire, but Juste Constant does not even refer to the matter. Benjamin, on his part, is incapable of uttering his carefully prepared apologies, despite the sincerity of his remorse. The relationship between the father and his son is poisoned at the core by the unconquerable timidity of both. The significance of this incident goes far beyond its obvious psychological interest, for in the framework of the *Cahier rouge* timidity is much more

[2] P. 134.

than a psychological problem: it is the very image and principle of the ultimate impossibility of communication between men. Expressing the essence of all the other misunderstandings, the scene between Juste and Benjamin assumes symbolic proportions. This episode is no longer humorous. Briefly but clearly it reveals a tragic note which is *secretly* present throughout the book: the realization of man's inescapable loneliness.

The amusing events can usually hide this aspect of the book, for misunderstanding can be seen in two perspectives. Viewed in a *subjective* context, it exemplifies the breakdown of human communication. Seen from the outside, however, from the point of view of "objective reality", it is a distorted picture of the true state of affairs. The novelist can detach himself from his subject, even if it is his own life, and occupy this objective point of vantage. In the *Cahier rouge* the essential tragedy of contorted communication is absorbed by the comedy of errors, in which reality is dissolved in the workings of caprice. Misunderstanding becomes just one expression of a pervasive insubstantiality of the real, which is the dominant note of the entire work. With consummate skill Constant conjures up a world where events, even though the protagonist is floating at their mercy, have a basic lack of solidity. Somehow reality seems to have lost the power of gravity. The climax is the fantastic Odyssey through England, which defies all the laws of common sense.

Benjamin's vagabondage through England is distinctly picaresque in both tone and content, and indeed the *Cahier rouge* as a whole is very much a picaresque novel. Perhaps there is an even closer parallel with Voltaire's "philosophical" adventure story, notably *Candide*, which is itself largely picaresque in technique. There is the same sober precision and rapidity of style, the same contraction of time. Above all, the novelistic world shows the same weightlessness which paradoxically enables a hero who is buffeted by the vicissitudes of fortune to move about as if he were not subject to the resistance of matter. This is a world where anything may happen and where nothing seems to be irrevocably serious. We see that the *Cahier rouge* is firmly grounded in the literary tradition of the eighteenth century. And rightly so, for the story is entirely set in the last decades of the Ancien Régime, when that period was singing its bewitchingly frivolous swan song. The protagonist's history merges with that of an era, and his frivolity reflects the spirit of the dying eighteenth century. Madame de Charrière, the most important character in the book next to the hero himself and his father, is almost a symbol of the Age of Reason. Witty, brilliant, vying with

34

the youth in mocking all beliefs and conventions, she is in effect the very personification of the hero's great temptation to dissolve all the apparent solidity of the surrounding world in the test-tube of the critical intellect.

However, the story has an additional dimension: that of memory. Constant wrote his book near the end of the Napoleonic era, and the air of unreality it exhales is *also* that of an historical epoch which has passed away, together with his youth. This note of nostalgia for the past already belongs to the nineteenth century. The very intensity of the problem of human communication is also a modern element. But both nostalgia and loneliness, both depth in time and subjective intensity, are absorbed by the picaresque technique: a specifically modern content is mastered by an older form. In this subtle way Constant's autobiography is a novel of transition.

Adolescence, Ancien Régime, eighteenth century novel, and ironically wistful memory: all these elements are fully integrated and fused into aesthetic unity. This unity could not have been maintained if Constant had continued the *Cahier rouge*. Events were soon to shatter its world: the French Revolution, with its overwhelming passion and tragedy, could not possibly bend itself to the picaresque tone. The same applies to

Madame de Staël's irruption into Constant's life, and even to his spiritual crisis during the Brunswick period. No doubt Constant set out to write the story of his *entire* life, but in his hands the material acquired novelistic structure and was transformed into literature. It is reasonable to assume that aesthetic considerations played a major role in determining the interruption of the work. Sooner or later the inner logic of narration will clash with the data of biography.

Cécile

It has been known for a long time that Constant wrote an unfinished autobiographical novel entitled *Cécile*, but until recently the manuscript seemed lost. In fact it was buried in one of the numerous cases with documents which he spread all over Europe in the course of his peregrinations. In the 1940's *Cécile* was found, and its publication in 1951 was a major literary event. The date of composition is uncertain, but may be 1811, as for the *Cahier rouge*.

In *Cécile*, as in the *Cahier rouge*, the narrator employs the first person singular. But now the names of the chief characters have been changed, which suggests that *Cécile* may have been conceived as a novel from the outset. Charlotte von Hardenberg, Constant's second wife, becomes Cécile de Walterbourg, while the Madame de

Malbée of the novel, "the most famous person of our century", is of course Madame de Staël. More important, Constant here does not depict his past, or any one period of his past, in its entirety. He confines himself to one particular subject, his relationship with Charlotte-Cécile, retracing its eventful history through the different periods of his life: their first liaison in Brunswick, their renewed acquaintance in Paris after many years of separation, and the unbelievable fluctuations of their entanglement with Madame de Staël. The account ends in December 1807 in the middle of a dangerous illness of the long-suffering Cécile, who has finally broken down under the strain. The work is divided into seven "epochs", each exactly dated. The widely differing relative length of these divisions, as well as of the periods they cover, is determined by the demands of the subject. One stretch of seven years, during which Charlotte played no role in Constant's life, has been entirely omitted. The subject requires an almost dramatic concentration, an elimination of all elements that do not contribute to the unfolding of the crucial theme. Thus time and action are entirely governed by one central line of development, and in the deforming mirror of this "autobiography", Constant's whole life appears as a gradual but certain progress towards the fated union with Cécile.

There is evidence that Constant slightly re-arranged the historical facts, and most certainly the characters cannot be completely identified with the actors in the real drama.[3] Literary reminiscences play a role in these modifications. The very title of the book was probably suggested by Madame de Charrière's novel *Lettres écrites de Lausanne*, where a Cécile is the heroine of the first part.

The almost exclusive concentration on the three principal characters underlines the dramatic quality of the narrative. The rapidly sketched characterization of Madame de Malbée, with her strangely indefinable charm, is a literary portrait in the tradition of French classicism. As the story develops, her authoritative, masculine side prevails and the heroine is clearly depicted as her polar opposite. Appropriately, Cécile's picture is vaguer than that of her more positive rival. Less a woman than a symbol of femininity, moving in an all-pervading aura of gentleness, Cécile is surely even sweeter and more angelically patient than the historical Charlotte. She is very much the passive, innocently victimized heroine of pre-

[3] On the literary transformations in *Cécile*, cf. Walter Pabst, "Die Stilisierung des literarischen Selbstporträts in Benjamin Constants *Cécile*", in *Formen der Selbstdarstellung, Analekten zu einer Geschichte der literarischen Selbstporträts*, Festgabe für Fritz Neubert, herausg. von Günter Reichenkron und Erich Haase (Berlin, 1956).

romantic literature, one of the numerous successors of Richardson's *Clarissa Harlowe*. The man who hurts her is as weak as the real Constant, and certainly even more cynical. The weak hero is another stock character in the novels of that period, but the narrator of *Cécile* can boast an additional dimension of odiousness. His hidden motives, generally disreputable, are completely transparent to his own scrutiny, and his matter-of-fact report of his actions is interwoven with an equally dispassionate disclosure of their secret mechanism. As in the *Cahier rouge*, self-judgment takes the indirect form of irony. But the irony of the *Cahier rouge* is a kind of perpetual amusement, light and devoid of bitterness. The tone of *Cécile*, however, is sardonic, and we gain the impression that the narrator views himself with detached and imperturbable disgust. In early December 1807 Madame de Malbée leaves for a trip, so that the protagonist can at last rejoin Cécile. Here are his feelings as he is relieved of his yoke: "Through a strange complication of diverse impressions, I regretted Madame de Malbée's departure precisely because I was grateful that she left. If she had suddenly decided to stay, all my impatience with her would have been revived. But certain as I was that soon I would be my own master again, I safely yielded to emotions of tenderness which were rendered even more sincere by their lack of consequence."[4] The irony seems to coincide with the sober correctness of the naked statement, it seems to spring from the inescapable dialectics of man's heart. The dominant note of this irony is a detached and impersonal contempt which, pointing beyond the hero of *Cécile*, is directed at every man's basic egoism. Thus the tone of the novel acquires a certain stateliness.

Again we are faced with the fact that Constant interrupted his book. This has been explained by the deterioration, in 1812, of his relationship with his wife. But there is a better hypothesis—better because internal to the work. "It was on 11 January 1793 that I first met Cécile de Walterbourg, now my wife"[5]: this is the first sentence of the book and it proves that he wanted to tell the pre-history of his *marriage*. But the growing dramatic intensity of the narrative prescribed a more tragic course. Significantly, the novel ends on a climax: Cécile lies near death in a small town inn. Does the internal logic of the work really permit her recovery, followed by a few more years of suffering and the final union of the lovers? Or was the author, reversing the facts, to bring about his heroine's death, thus duplicating the story of Ellénore in *Adolphe*? Was he to sacrifice truth to fiction or fiction to truth? Even

[4] P. 213.   [5] P. 171.

more clearly than the *Cahier rouge*, *Cécile* reveals the pitfalls of autobiography, the irreducible gap between life and its literary representation.

Adolphe

In its essentials *Adolphe* was written as early as 1806, although it remained unpublished until 1816. In placing the book after the *Cahier rouge* and *Cécile*, I therefore do not follow chronology: the sequence of discussion is determined by the degree of literary transformation, of *stylization* of the biographical material. *Adolphe* is the only novel which Constant actually completed. Here the autobiographer has entirely transformed himself into a novelist, i.e. he has detached himself from his life and transcended it in a finished work of art. In this respect, *Adolphe* is a unique accomplishment for Constant, and it is probable that the writing of his later books was at least partly prompted by the desire to repeat this cathartic achievement.

Adolphe is also Constant's only novel which appeared during his lifetime. It soon gained an important place in standard histories of literature, which usually treat it as a classic example of the French novel of psychological analysis, more or less in the line of Madame de Lafayette's *Princesse de Clèves*.

The narrative is introduced by the familiar

"fiction", which had already become a stereotype: Constant pretends that he met the mysterious Adolphe in the course of his travels and is publishing the stranger's manuscript, which is written in the form of a confession. It is the story of a man whose weakness, indecision, and egoism have killed the woman who loved him. At a small German Court Adolphe meets Ellénore, who comes from an impoverished family of Polish nobility and is the acknowledged mistress of Monsieur de P . . . In trying to seduce this woman, who is ten years his senior, he actually falls in love with her. Soon after he has conquered her, however, his ardour begins to cool and he becomes more and more reasonable: Ellénore is no longer a goal, she has become a bond. But Ellénore's love for Adolphe grows until she finally leaves Monsieur de P . . . and the two children she has had with him, thus sacrificing a situation of relative respectability. Adolphe, who becomes increasingly tired of Ellénore's love, decides to visit his home town, but promises to rejoin her after two months. The letters he writes her are lukewarm, and when he finally tries to delay his return, she follows him in person. At their reunion the two lovers have one of a long series of terrible scenes. But when Adolphe learns that his father has taken steps to have Ellénore expelled from the town, he flees

with her to Bohemia. With unfailing certainty of
touch, Constant now describes the successive
stages of their deteriorating relationship. Pity
rather than love has induced Adolphe to leave
with his mistress, and soon his liaison weighs on
him like slavery. Basically indifferent, but re-
morseful about his indifference, then again angry
about his remorse, he is continually torn between
the extremes of irritation and pity. His one weak
attempt at a rupture throws Ellénore into such a
paroxysm of suffering that he does not dare to
repeat the suggestion. Ellénore herself becomes
bitter, and the atmosphere is further poisoned by
the disapproval of respectable society, so that
quarrels multiply and increase in violence.
Nevertheless, when Ellénore's property in Poland
is restored to her through a political reversal,
Adolphe goes to live with her on one of her
estates. She now makes pathetic and hopeless
efforts to regain his affection, at one point even
trying to provoke his jealousy. Meanwhile
Adolphe frequents the French ambassador in
Warsaw, Baron de T . . ., a friend of his father
and the very personification of the ways and
opinions of society, who tries to detach him from
Ellénore. In a weak moment Adolphe promises
the Baron to break with her, and he is imprudent
enough to reaffirm this promise in a letter. When
he still hesitates, the Baron sends this letter to

43

Ellénore, who immediately collapses with a violent fever. Weighed down by remorse and by a sudden fear of loneliness, Adolphe, who desperately begs Ellénore's forgiveness, must helplessly watch the process of her rapid decay. After her death he discovers a letter which reproaches him for the cruelty of his weakness, revealing the full depth of her suffering and the extent of his guilt.

This is the bare outline of the story, and its obvious autobiographical elements have been discussed *ad infinitum*. The basic situation is clearly inspired by Constant's relations with Madame de Staël. On the other hand, Ellénore's passionate, feminine character is reminiscent of Anna Lindsay; so is her social position at the beginning of the book. Traits of Charlotte and (as a literary source) of Caliste, a character in the previously mentioned novel by Madame de Charrière, also contribute to the heroine's portrait. Ellénore's illness and death is a combination of Charlotte's breakdown and Julie Talma's death. The cosmopolitan, blasé Adolphe of the beginning resembles the young Constant of the early Brunswick period. His adolescence, just like Constant's, has been marked by two dominating influences: that of his father, with whom he had a precarious relationship marred by mutual timidity, and that of an "elderly woman" with a sharply critical mind in whom we recognize

Madame de Charrière. Such parallels could be multiplied, and yet the book is by no means a mosaic of incoherent elements. All these biographical components have been welded into artistic unity and are merged in a whole that is no longer Constant's life.

At its appearance, *Adolphe* was received as a "romantic" novel, a description which seems justified by the very fact that it has the character of a *confession*. The hapless Adolphe, who exhibits his guilt with such frankness, has quickly taken his place in literary history as a brother of other early romantic heroes who are equally sombre and unhappy, such as Goethe's Werther, Chateaubriand's René, Sénancour's Obermann, and certain Byronic figures. Constant's protagonist starts out as a would-be seducer in the eighteenth-century tradition, but he falls into his own trap and is overwhelmed by the passion he seeks to inspire. The value placed on *feeling*, so great that its absence is criminal, is a distinctly romantic element; so is the haunting awareness of the transitoriness of passion, the horror of death and solitude, and above all the exaltation of love as against the narrow-minded conventions and sordid calculations of society. Adolphe's obsession with human pain is so strong that Constant has been credited with a "religion of suffering". Before its publication,

45

Constant used to read *Adolphe* aloud at social gatherings. The success of these readings prove its emotional appeal to his contemporaries: the listeners wept so profusely that Constant, himself in tears, often found it difficult to proceed.

And yet the tone of *Adolphe* could hardly be less "romantic". Indeed, poetically-minded critics have accused the work of being drab and depressing. There is none of the effusive lyricism which is displayed on every page of Chateaubriand's *René*. The imagery is scarce and controlled. The style—rapid, bare, and self-effacing —seems to aim at nothing but brief and exact formulation. Descriptions of nature are rare and avoid the picturesque: the winter landscape in which Adolphe and Ellénore take their last walk is a perfect image of the approaching end. With supreme economy of means, each element is reduced to the essential function of illuminating the central theme and pushing it towards its *dénouement*. The general sobriety, coupled with the limpidity of form, places the novel in the tradition of French classicism. The depiction of the characters is reminiscent of the classicist *portrait*: characterizations are sketched in a few precise and rapid lines, physical descriptions are scarce and unobtrusive. *Adolphe* was composed at a time when the classicist tradition, which had governed the French literary scene ever since the seventeenth century, was beginning to be shaken by the romantic onslaught. The successful fusion of classicist and romantic elements makes this novel a rarely perfect work of transition.

Just as in *Cécile*, the psychological mechanism of the characters seems to hold no secrets, and its workings are revealed in bare and dispassionate statements. Yet here the atmosphere is not one of contemptuous irony, but rather of contained melancholy. The keynote of the work is the moral and psychological aphorism: "We are such changeable creatures that we end up by experiencing the feelings which we feign". Such concise and usually pessimistic observations on human nature, which might have been written by La Rochefoucauld, continually illustrate the story without ever interrupting its progression. These *aperçus* contribute to create an impression of *universality* which is further enhanced by a kind of abstract cosmopolitanism, a complete lack of local colour. The reader feels that in a sense he is following the history of *every* love, but unadorned by illusion and pushed to its extreme conclusion. The problem of human communication is insoluble and the individual remains imprisoned in his loneliness. When Adolphe, shortly before Ellénore's death, reflects that he is going "to live without her in this desert of the world", this is much more than the self-pity of an objectionable individual: it is the sudden realization of man's situation in the universe.

Yet it must be admitted that there is something peculiarly disagreeable in the atmosphere of the book. Of course, this impression of unpleasantness springs from the pitiless lucidity with which Adolphe reveals his weakness, his indecision, and his fundamental lack of generosity. But Adolphe's lucidity does not only *expose* his faults, it is also their ultimate *cause*. Adolphe is incapable of *real* love, he cannot entirely devote himself to anything, for self-observation divides him and prevents all spontaneity. His will and his feelings are stymied by his critical intellect. Self-division in some form is one of the symptoms of the romantic *mal du siècle*, but Adolphe's version of that sickness is free of the sentimentality which characterizes most heroes of the early nineteenth century novel. Perhaps none has remained as modern as *Adolphe*.

Constant has left one more autobiographical document of an entirely different nature.

The Journaux intimes[6]

Constant did not write his intimate journals for publication and never even mentioned their

[6] I developed the following ideas on the intimate journals of Benjamin Constant in an essay, entitled "Benjamin Constant et ses *Journaux intimes*", published in the *Cahiers des Saisons* of spring 1960.

existence to any of his friends. They constitute an authentic diary, and not one of those instruments which authors sometimes use in order to fashion their public image. They first appeared in a truncated version with misleading changes and even arbitrary additions. Only since 1952 does a reliable edition exist. Four *Journaux* have come down to us. The first, which is entitled *Amélie et Germaine* and comprises the early months of 1803, is entirely devoted to Constant's trepidations regarding a possible marriage with a Genevese girl, Amélie Fabri, a match which would allow him to escape from Germaine de Staël's yoke. The second (January 1804–May 1805), which presents the most immediate psychological, documentary, and literary interest, begins during the trip to Germany with Madame de Staël and ends shortly after Julie Talma's death in Paris. The *Journal abrégé* (January 1804–December 1807), largely in telegram style and partly in code, extends to the tormented years of oscillation between Madame de Staël and Charlotte von Hardenberg-Dutertre. The last *Journal* (May 1811–September 1816), also abridged in part and originally written in Greek characters, throws light on Constant's political role during the early Restoration and on his unhappy love for Madame Récamier.

The journal is a favoured genre in our time,

since it allows us to follow the diarist day by day, creating the illusion that we are face to face with the man himself. For its human interest alone, Constant's contribution would be an outstanding specimen of this type of literature. Moreover, the authentic personal flavour, coupled with Constant's habitual brilliance and clarity of style, makes its reading a rewarding experience. It is rarely a cheerful document: the reader senses Constant's eternal fear of causing pain, his awareness of the passing of time, his obsession with death, and his tormenting indecision. The judgments on people, events, and works of literature and scholarship, penetrating and often spiced with delightful irony, again and again crystallize into those pithy and perfectly formulated *aperçus* which make Constant a successor of the seventeenth century French moralists.

Like most diarists, Constant is concerned with the mystery of his own self. ". . . this Journal is a kind of history, and I need my history . . . in order not to forget and lose myself all the time" (21 December 1804): he wants to grasp the continuity of the self below the unceasing flux of changing impressions. There is nothing new in this, but it is Constant who has pushed the dialectics of this quest to their ultimate conclusion.

He is far removed from the Rousseauistic pretension of showing "a man in all the truth of nature". In fact he knows that complete sincerity is impossible and that his image of himself will be slanted. "I must record here that I treat my Journal like my life," he writes on 17 October 1804. "I register my sorrows much more than my pleasures." Two months later he complains that the fatal habit of "speaking for the gallery" sometimes prevents him from observing the self-imposed rule of noting all his feelings.[7] Does one not always write for a public, even if this public is oneself?

It is commonly assumed that Constant's journal is a classic document of self-analysis. This view is based on the reputation of the man and on certain preconceived ideas about the genre (for in a journal, after all, one is supposed to "analyze oneself"), but is not supported by a careful reading of the text. No doubt the ambiguity of the word "analysis" has also favoured this error. It is true that an "analysis" may be nothing more than a summary, a mere enumeration; this meaning is contained even more clearly in the French equivalent, "une analyse". But surely in a literary context the term denotes an active exploration, a conscious attempt at clarification. The important thing in a literary analysis is the *active* interference of an analyzing mind. What is truly surprising in Constant's diary is the

[7] 18 December 1804.

fact that his quest for self involves only a bare minimum of real self-exploration. There is some, but very little of that eternal questioning (centering on the query "Who am I?") which is so striking in the journals of Amiel or Gide. The inner tendency of this diary, excepting the early *Amélie et Germaine* episode, increasingly moves towards the simple statement of fact. "I must *record* . . .", "I *register* my sorrows . . ."—the terminology is revealing: this is not analysis, but book-keeping. Without omitting a day, avoiding all selectiveness, Constant tries to catalogue everything. Sensations, thoughts, judgments, reminiscences, letters received and written, plans to arrange his life: all are painstakingly recorded and put on the same level of "factuality".

The abbreviated sections of the diary are of cardinal importance because they represent the ideal limit of this tendency. Desire for secrecy or lack of time cannot completely account for these abridgements, especially if we consider that the beginning of the *Journal abrégé* overlaps with the preceding one, thus entirely *restating* it in an abbreviated version. Already in his full-length Journal Constant declares that he does not want to re-live his impressions, but only to remember *that* he experienced them. The abridged version tends to eliminate all subjective elements and to reduce biography to a succession of bare facts.

Its ideal limit is the statement in its pure form. As an example, here is the entry for 25 May 1805: "4. 2. Dinner with Hochet. Evening at Mme Gay's. Letter from Mme de Staël. 2. 2. 2. 2. 2. 2. 12. 12. 12. 1." Fortunately for us, Constant has left the key to the code. *1* stands for physical pleasure, *2* for the wish to break with Madame de Staël, while *4* and *12* mean, respectively, "work" and "love for Madame Dutertre". Altogether there are seventeen such figures, and among others their meanings include the temporary revival of affection for Madame de Staël, marriage plans, hesitations concerning Madame Dutertre, and uncertainty about everything. Thus emotions are not completely eliminated from the *Journal abrégé*, but are maintained in the form of symbols which endow them with statistical coldness and objectivity. Even where symbols do not replace words, linguistic expression is stripped and reduced to a minimum. The numerical code is the final step, for it transcends language towards an algebra of the soul.

All linguistic formulation entails a falsification, for it constitutes an intervention of the writer. Here we touch upon the intrinsic paradox of self-description. The writer changes in the very act of observing and describing himself, even if he shuns the more active intervention of self-analysis and the subjectivism of emotion. In moving away from language, Constant's journal seeks the precision and objectivity of mathematical formulation. In the very act of observing himself Constant paradoxically tries to eliminate himself as an observer. It is as if he hoped that the abridged form, so easy to survey, will *by itself* unveil the inner pattern of his life. He has written the journal *par excellence*, which illuminates the paradox inherent in this genre. The logic of the journal, as an instrument of self-exploration, ultimately leads to the rejection of language: it is the literary genre which must try to cancel itself.

But this anti-literary, anti-subjective trend, which ultimately tends to reduce individual experience to a succession of quantitatively measurable symbols, cannot be consistently maintained. Thus the incursion of passion (first for Charlotte, later for Madame Récamier) always changes the character of this diary, plunging it again into the subjectivism of linguistic expression: the sentences become longer, the rhythm fuller, the tone emotional. At such times Constant's desire for "theoretical" self-knowledge is overpowered by his need of emotional catharsis. Therefore the consciously anti-literary tendency of the later journals rarely reaches its extreme limit.

What has been said about Constant's diaries does not apply to the first Journal, *Amélie et Germaine*, which is a continual *analysis* of one specific problem: Constant's relations with Amélie Fabri. The entries are confined to the days when this problem occupied his mind. In form this is a journal, but potentially it is a story built around a central theme. The *Amélie et Germaine* fragment was undoubtedly inspired by the desire to clarify a difficult situation, but consciously or unconsciously it gropes its way towards the literary stylization of *Adolphe* and *Cécile*. Ultimately these notes of early 1803 move towards an ideal of language and form, and not towards self-knowledge and truth.

But is not *truth* a quality of the novels, and their purpose? Impressed by the dispassionate clarity of *Adolphe*, the critic Charles Du Bos has described this novel as "the masterpiece of the statement of fact". In both *Adolphe* and *Cécile*, however, the seemingly factual account of actions and events always conceals their analysis: the "statement of fact" is a hidden interpretation. The narrator can create the illusion of perfect objectivity, although he tells the story of his own life, because he is also the author of a novel and shares the author's fictional detachment. A diarist who analyzes himself remains plunged in life, in the stream of *becoming*, where nothing is ever finished. His questioning is perpetual and the answer will always elude him. But in *Adolphe* and *Cécile* the narrator is like a god who hovers above a realm which *is what it is*, "objectively" and for all times, a world where everything is clear and defined. It is a world of *fiction*, no matter how much it may resemble the author's life.

And the *Cahier rouge*? To be sure, its picaresque atmosphere is different from the contemptuous irony of *Cécile* and the aphoristic universality of *Adolphe*. Yet even here we find the narrator's withdrawal into fictional "objectivity". The subjective problem of isolation and timidity is reduced to the "objective" fact of misunderstanding, subjective intensity is absorbed by "objective" motion in space: emotion becomes commotion. In the *Cahier rouge* the narrator withdraws into the playful detachment of sheer amusement. In *Adolphe* and *Cécile* he turns into the uncommitted, omniscient observer and recorder of a story which may be full of anguish and division, but which has the harmony, unattainable in life, of a thing closed in itself, finished and explained. The "explanation" belongs to the sphere of literature, not to the sphere of cognition: Constant has transcended not only his life, but also his urge to elucidate his life, by integrating both in the realm of fiction. In writing his novels he found catharsis rather than truth.

The problem of "sincerity", the quest for the individual's genuine being, has been haunting Western thought and literature ever since Rousseau. Therefore it is hardly surprising that the apparent frankness of Constant's writings has been one of the reasons for their popularity. Many critics have praised Constant's "sincerity" in his novels, while others have called it in question. Both judgments are equally beside the point. In the domain of the novel, "falsifications" are not vices but literary transpositions. Sincerity itself is not an ethical but an aesthetic quality which serves to endow the work with an additional dimension. The atmosphere of "veracity" which characterizes Constant's autobiographical novels is not a virtue, but an artistic device.

III

TRAGEDY AND SOCIETY

The Literary Critic

Constant wrote few other works of literary importance. *Le Siège de Soissons*, a satirical anti-Napoleonic poem disguised as a romance of chivalry, merely proves his ineptitude as a poet. Two more prose works are at least worth mentioning: first of all the "Lettre sur Julie", a beautiful homage to Julie Talma written shortly after her death but published only in 1829 in a collection of essays entitled *Mélanges de littérature et de politique*, and secondly, the fragmentary *Mémoires*, to which I have already referred and which contain, in addition to the "récit de Juliette", well-written literary portraits of such contemporaries as Sieyès and Talleyrand.

Constant, versatile as he was, also wrote some literary criticism. Though his place in the history of criticism is not particularly important, his contribution is more significant than would appear at first sight. Most of his critical writings are collected in the *Mélanges*.

As a critic Constant may be considered a transitional figure. Although he expresses the beginnings of a liberation from traditional classicist standards of judgment, he is basically still a classicist in taste, as appears from his essay "De la littérature dans ses rapports avec la liberté", in which he duly deplores the "coarse expressions" in Sallust's and Lucretius' works and declares that Plautus' comical force "does not excuse his coarseness".[1] The elegance and aesthetic purity of the classical Augustan period remain Constant's criterion of excellence, and he sees the subsequent evolution of Roman literature as a process of degeneration. He wrote the essay to counter a favourite contention of the reactionary royalists of the French Restoration period who argued that the golden ages of Augustus and Louis XIV prove the superiority of absolutism as a breeding ground for literary excellence. By demonstrating that the prominent "Augustans" fully developed their talents either before the emperor's absolute rule or in spite of it, Constant wants to refute this argument of his political opponents and at the same time to reconcile his aristocratic literary taste with his political liberalism.

According to the preface of the *Mélanges*, freedom is the central idea which unifies all these

[1] Cf. pp. 889 and 890.

essays, "freedom in everything, in religion, in philosophy, in literature, in industry, in politics".[2] Indeed, Constant played a part in the revolt against the constraints imposed upon French tragedy, that chief bastion of classicist doctrinaire thinking. In 1809 he published an unsuccessful adaptation of Schiller's historical drama *Wallenstein* for the French stage. In the preface to his *Wallstein* he warned against the threatening asphyxiation of French tragedy through the tyranny of antiquated rules, condemning above all the crippling demand for unity of time and place. This manifesto, in which Constant was more or less the spokesman for the Coppet group, became an important landmark in French criticism. However, it was not really revolutionary: the eighteenth-century *philosophe* Diderot had already attacked the unities of time and place. Constant re-worked his preface for the *Mélanges* (1829), adding an enlightening criticism of his own version of Schiller's play. He admits that in practice he has been too timid, reducing Schiller's vigorous dramatic trilogy to a bloodless play which respects most of the traditional standards of French tragedy. Yet even now he does not wish to go too far. The movement of liberation he prudently helped to create has gained momentum

[2] P. 835.

and found bolder expression in Victor Hugo's preface to *Cromwell* (1827). The historical drama is favoured now, and the rejection of all rules has become a commonplace. The iconoclastic zeal of the new romantic school has led to excesses which shock Constant's aristocratic temperament. He feels that the young group tends to overstep the bounds of "truth", that its art is often "unnatural" and "tasteless" (all these terms come from the classicist arsenal!), and he looks forward to the time when the new liberties will be used in a more judicious way.

Occasionally Constant likes to relate literary works to their sociological context. Here again he is no pioneer: the trend comes from the Montesquieu tradition, and the eighteenth-century writer Marmontel had engaged in this type of criticism. Madame de Staël had done the same in her books *De la littérature* and *De l'Allemagne*, and Constant's article on literature in relation to liberty is in effect a more erudite treatment of a problem she had taken up in the latter work. But Constant uses the sociological approach with moderation and never in any systematic way. It serves him to clarify some aspects of a writer but never leads to the sweeping generalizations in which Madame de Staël loved to indulge, or to the levelling relativism of the later nineteenth century. Constant was too perceptive a connoisseur of literature, he stood too close to the aesthetic essence of a work, to succumb to these temptations. In this as in other matters, his sagacity of judgment rarely failed him, and when in his "Réflexions sur la tragédie" he blames the "bombast" and "false exaltation" of Diderot's plays, we feel that he cannot have been blind to similar faults in the style of his friend, "the most famous woman of the century".

In an otherwise unimportant essay on Madame de Staël and her novel *Corinne*, Constant declares that the contemplation of beauty detaches the observer from himself. This is clearly an echo of the Kantian theory which defines the aesthetic emotion as "disinterested pleasure". Constant's familiarity with the German language, his profound understanding of contemporary developments in German thought and letters, account for numerous traces of German influence in his writings on literature. In the *Wallstein* preface we find some remarks about Schiller's secondary characters who, contrary to the "confidents" of French tragedy, lead a life of their own. They are spectators of the chief action, mediators between stage and public. Constant points out that the ancient chorus established a similar "moral correspondence" between the spectators and the world of the tragedy, and analyzes Schiller's experiment with a chorus in the *Braut von Messina*.

All this makes Constant the critic a brilliant and sensitive dilettante who was exposed to the currents of his time, but not a major force in the history of criticism. His one work which shows truly powerful originality was ignored and completely forgotten for more than a century. I am referring to the "Réflexions sur la tragédie", which appeared in the *Revue de Paris* in 1829 and was not republished until recently. This important essay contains nothing less than a re-examination of the concept of tragedy. Its point of departure is a critique of Diderot's theories on domestic tragedy. Diderot's idea of replacing character by social condition is superficial, but it points in the direction of a deeper and more fruitful thought. Every tragedy hinges on the conflict between an inner force and an external obstacle, and in modern drama it has always been the former which has primacy. This inner force may be the total configuration of the tragic hero's strong and rich personality (the "tragedy of character"), or it may be a single overpowering passion that governs him (the "tragedy of passion"). Constant contends that both these forms of tragedy have exhausted their resources and that the individual can no longer be primary in a period in which the masses have become conscious of their existence. The drama of the future is the "tragedy of society". In the plays of the past, society has never been more than a framework, but now it must come to occupy the central place. The depiction of a complex social system of laws, institutions, and interrelations which oppresses and finally crushes the individual offers new dramatic possibilities.

The "Réflexions sur la tragédie" appeared when the romantic movement was in process of capturing the French stage. No wonder that the essay found no echo! Constant is too far ahead of the romantic individualism of his time. His remarks are inspired by a play of the German writer Robert, an immediate precursor of the liberal literary group "Young Germany", and his dramatic theory definitely foreshadows the naturalist drama of the late nineteenth century. But the new *tragic feeling* he describes will perhaps be more perfectly expressed in the work of Georg Büchner, that great writer who passes like a meteor, only a few years after Constant's death.

Man and Society[3]

I spoke of a "new tragic feeling", for Constant's theory is inspired by an authentic sense of tragedy. His involvement in politics might make

[3] Some of the ideas in the following section and in the next chapter were developed in a paper on "Benjamin Constant and the Problem of the Modern Personality" which was presented on 29 December 1959 in Chicago, at the meeting of the *Modern Language Association*.

us fear that his "tragedy of society" is really nothing but a didactic theatre with a political tendency, but he is much too discerning a critic to content himself with such a superficial view. In fact, he criticizes the plays of Diderot and Voltaire ("the Euripides of France") for their propagandistic tendency. Such didactic effects are not those of tragedy—they are "foreign to its nature and detrimental to its perfection".[4] What he has in mind is a return to the original source of tragedy, the Aeschylean drama of "situation". However, since we are far removed from the metaphysics of ancient Greece, society must take the place of fate.

The social order in its impact on the individual is "entirely equivalent to the fatality of the ancients".[5] Its oppressive power shapes his life, and the modern spectator will shudder at its omnipotence as the ancient shuddered at the horror of Nemesis. The social system is much more than a mere conglomerate of material forces: it is our modern Aeschylean Curse, a power of metaphysical dimensions and significance. Man, blind and feeble, is "without his knowledge and consent thrown into this labyrinth called the world", and it surrounds him with an intricate maze of institutions and

[4] P. 942, in the "Réflexions sur la tragédie".
[5] P. 952, in the "Réflexions sur la tragédie".

conventions which "weigh on him like a pre-existing burden" he never accepted to carry.[6] Here Constant's language takes on accents of vibrant emotion, the very terms he uses remind us of existentialist descriptions of man's fate, and we feel that we are near the vital core of his thought. The problem of man in relation to society is indeed a recurrent, almost an obsessive theme throughout his work. It has such crucial importance that it must be specially analyzed.

The key lies in the expression "to create an impact" (*faire effet*), a stock phrase which recurs repeatedly under Constant's pen. Thus on several occasions he reflects that perhaps the French needed the old classicist rules more than any other nation. The French want to create an impact at all costs so that they speak, write, and act only for the "others". In the German character there is a basic scrupulousness which keeps the imagination within certain bounds. But the French dramatists, if unrestrained by rules, will stop at no extravagance in their desire to impress the public. Constant likes to make comparisons between the French and the German character, and naturally he does not always favour the German side. However, vanity and the urge to "create an impact" are invariably stressed as French characteristics.

[6] Cf. p. 944, in the "Réflexions sur la tragédie".

This line of reasoning is not confined to aesthetic questions. In fact, it is carried to the extreme in a passage of the *Principes de politique* (1815). In France, Constant writes, the urge to create an impact is the chief menace to both order and freedom. It is all the more dangerous "because it is not grounded in human nature, but is a social creation, the late and factitious product of an old civilization and of a huge capital city". Truth as against falsity, human nature as against society: the very terminology reminds us of Jean-Jacques Rousseau. Indeed one can hardly fail to be struck by the Rousseauistic side of a man who is capable of noting in his diary that he dislikes witty women, since they are a social and *consequently* an artificial creation (9 February 1804). The desire to *shine* (Constant proceeds in the *Principles*) grows irresistibly, and not even fatigue can weaken it, since the individual never consults his own sensations but only those he produces in others. "Opinions, eloquence, emotions—all these are means, and the whole man is transformed into a tool of his own vanity."[7] There can be no clearer statement of the doctrine of *alienation*, as it appears in Rousseau's "Second Discourse". By living in society, man is distorted at the core, in his innermost being. He becomes "alienated" from himself (the

[7] Cf. the whole passage on pp. 1155-6.

67

term occurs in Rousseau's treatise) until he loses his very identity and has no more existence of his own. In this final stage of self-estrangement, social man literally lives "outside" himself, in a realm of seeming rather than being, drawing all consciousness of his existence from the opinions of the "others".

In the Journal of 15 April 1804, the key phrase "to create an impact" occurs in still another revealing context: "Euripides is a completely modern poet, i.e., he has none of the simplicity, the good faith, the sincerity of the ancients. He is addicted to the idea of creating an impact. . . ." Already Schiller declares that the "naïveté" of ancient Greek poetry begins to disappear in Euripides. Indeed the whole distinction between the ancients and the moderns which is implied in Constant's Journal entry, and which reappears in many of his writings, has its source in the sphere of the German "classicist" aesthetics of Friedrich Schiller and the early Friedrich Schlegel, with its glorification of the ancients.

Constant often refers to the weakness and complication of modern man. Once he writes: "In *Adolphe* I wanted to depict one of the chief maladies of our time: that weariness, that uncertainty, that lack of strength, that perpetual analysis which places a mental reservation beside all feelings, corrupting them from the outset. . . . We have become incapable of loving, believing, and willing."[8] Contemporary man is weakened and divided in himself by the hypertrophy of reflective reason. Constant's concept of the modern personality is strongly reminiscent of Schiller's analysis in the letters "Über die ästhetische Erziehung des Menschen" (1795) and in the essay "Über naive und sentimentalische Dichtung" (1795–6), which contain a theory of alienation. According to Schiller's view, men have become fragments, cut off from nature and at odds with themselves, without unity of thought and feeling. The "sentimental" poet longs to recapture the ideal harmony and to reunite consciously what has been separated. Let us add the young Friedrich Schlegel's description of modern poetry as artificial, unharmonious, philosophical, as a poetry which merely seeks striking, individual, "interesting" effects and reflects the confusion and dividedness of modern man.[9] To these ideas Constant gives a Rousseauistic slant, thus amalgamating Rousseau's ontology

[8] Passage written for the preface of *Adolphe*, but later omitted. Quoted in French by Edward D. Sullivan in "Constraint and Expansion in Benjamin Constant's *Adolphe*", *The French Review*, XXXII, No. 4 (February 1959), 294–5.

[9] Cf. especially Friedrich Schlegel's early essays "Über die Grenzen des Schönen" (1794) and "Über das Studium der griechischen Poesie" (1795–6).

and German aesthetic theory. We have been falsified to the core by the process of social self-estrangement, and if we are severed from nature and fragmented within ourselves it is because we continually observe ourselves in order to control the impression we make on others. The rift between being and appearing, diagnosed by Rousseau, is the key to the debilitating complexity of modern man.

Constant's thought revolves around a double polarization: the opposition between the French and the Germans and that between the ancients and the moderns. How are these categories related to each other? Clearly the French are construed as the *modern* nation *par excellence*. But the Germans are by no means present-day equivalents of the ancient Greeks. As all modern men, they are divided within themselves and severed from objective reality. The harmonious union between subject and object has become impossible: only by accepting and accenting our separation from the world, by exalting our inner truth against the falseness and corruption of our surroundings, can we return to some measure of authenticity. In a supreme quest for *sincerity* the individual can crash through his own ambiguities and falsities and penetrate to the genuine, pristine elements of his being. Here lies the exemplary significance of the Germans, who have "a profound natural sensibility".[10] Constant believes, or tries to believe, that feeling is sincere. Unblemished by society, it springs from man's true nature. This is the point where Constant comes closest to the Romanticists, whom he resembles when he extols "enthusiasm" and the sanctity of passion. "I never knew a woman before I knew you," he writes to Anna Lindsay. "All those I met were either degraded and corrupted or at least warped and distorted by society. You alone are the ideal beauty of feminine nature."[11] Ellénore in *Adolphe* is genuine in her devotion to her passion. Society crushes her not only through the pressure of public opinion, but more effectively through the havoc it has wrought in her lover's nature, which is torn, complicated, fragmentary. The self-searching Adolphe is incapable of true "enthusiasm".

Though Constant has been credited with some fashionable literary Rousseauism, he is usually considered an intellectual descendant of the more "orthodox" sections of the eighteenth-century "philosophical movement". But his Rousseauism is much more than a mere vague emotional orientation: it is a contributing factor to the precise formulation of a consistent intellectual

[10] Cf. p. 917, in the revised *Wallstein* article.

[11] *Correspondance de Benjamin Constant et d'Anna Lindsay*, publiée par la Baronne Constant de Rebecque (Paris, 1933), p. 29. Letter of 25 December 1800.

doctrine. He is influenced by nothing less than Rousseau's central tenet, which the *philosophes*, with their essential faith in sociability, could not accept! Rousseau sees the problem of alienation exclusively in terms of the rococo society in which he lived. Constant, aided no doubt by certain German analyses, applies it to the realities of modern life, where politics takes on far greater and more fateful significance. Constant is after all not quite unjustified in choosing France as a symbol of modernity: in many respects the modern era *did* begin in France, and the old *salon* society was already in process of being supplanted by a much more oppressive social structure. The France of the revolutionary and imperial eras is in fact an adumbration, and more, of the mammoth mass state. Man, already corrupt and voided of his substance, is entirely at the mercy of this monolith. At this point Constant's individualism takes on tragic dimensions. Did not Napoleon himself say that politics is the modern form of fate?

We see that it is not Constant's interest in politics which dictates his ideas in the "Réflexions sur la tragédie". It would be more correct to say that it is his sense of modern tragedy which underlies his political doctrine, for Constant's tragic view of man and society is the philosophical basis of his liberalism.

IV

THE POLITICIAN AND POLITICAL THEORIST

Constant's Political Life

It is now almost forgotten that in his time Constant was a political theoretician of international repute and, next to Bentham, the most widely-read liberal in Europe. His influence reached as far as Russia, was particularly potent in Italy, and in Poland there was a liberal group called the "Benjaminists". Not only his writings but also his active participation in French political life contributed to spreading his fame. He was not an abstract political thinker who evolved his ideas in detachment, but theory and practice went together in continual interaction.

Constant's sympathies were from the outset on the side of revolutionary France, but he abhorred the Terror regime of the Jacobins. His political career began in 1795, when he arrived in Paris with Madame de Staël. Like his famous friend, who engaged in untiring political intrigue and used her influence in his favour, Constant supported the group of republicans around Barras and, after some vacillation, declared for the Constitution of the year III, which established the Directoire.

The situation was uneasy, for the moderate republicanism of Barras was in danger of being crushed between the two extremes: the left-wing "Terroristic" Jacobins and the reactionary royalists. Constant became very active as a writer and journalist, defending the Government and attacking the extremist groups. Thus in two pamphlets of 1797, "Des réactions politiques" and "Des effets de la Terreur", he tried to refute the arguments by which the Terror was defended, and pleaded with the Jacobins to support the Government. Constant's chief concern in those years was the preservation of the republican form of government. His "Essai sur la contre-révolution d'Angleterre en 1660" (1798) conjures up the frightening spectre of Restoration, drawing a vivid picture of counter-revolutionary terror. Constant went so far as to defend the *coup d'état* of 18 *fructidor*, which Barras carried out against two other ruling Directors. Later, when Constant had become the declared enemy of all violations of legality, he condemned Barras's act of violence, and his enemies lost no opportunity of attacking his earlier ambiguous attitude.

The Government did little to reward Constant

for his support. The left-wing Jacobin press violently attacked him for his aristocratic origin and for his relations with the meddlesome Madame de Staël. Another delicate issue, which was to be raised a second time during the Restoration, was Constant's foreign birth. On both occasions he could refer to a law of 1790 which gave French citizenship to all descendants of French subjects who had ever left the country under the pressure of religious or political persecution. This time the question was automatically settled, in 1798, when Constant's birthplace was annexed by France. However, he did not succeed in entering the "Corps législatif" as representative for Geneva.

Yet he moved in influential circles. He was one of the founders and the secretary of the "Cercle Constitutionnel", called "Club de Salm", whose members included Talleyrand and Sieyès. Constant also stood close to the *Décade*, the organ of the so-called "Idéologues", who were the intellectual descendants and continuers of the eighteenth century "philosophical movement". These theorists applied the analytical methods of Condillac's sensationalist psychology to the social sciences, with the aim of accelerating progress and bringing about a rational organization of society. Their outlook was republican, anticlerical, bourgeois, and anti-Jacobin; during the

Terror they had generally sided with the moderate Girondins. They more or less embodied the ideological basis of the Directoire, during which they played an important political role and exerted considerable influence on legislation. Constant frequented the *salon* of Helvétius' widow, which was the social centre of the group, and was well acquainted with leading Idéologues such as Daunou (who had drawn up the Constitution of the year III), Cabanis, Destutt de Tracy, Garat, and Ginguené.

Under the Consulate he remained closely associated with these republican bourgeois intellectuals. Together with several of their group he became a member of the Tribunate, which was a purely advisory body. There he showed courage in opposing the growing dictatorial ambitions of the First Consul Bonaparte. The latter had first been on good terms with the Idéologues, but when he felt their resistance he became increasingly hostile, branding them as cloudy metaphysicians and impractical intellectuals. At the end of 1801 he finally removed the whole group, including Constant, from the Tribunate, thus eradicating the last traces of true republicanism.

Bonaparte's dictatorship put an end to Constant's political activity for more than a decade. Only after Napoleon's Russian campaign did

Constant, who was then living in Germany, re-enter the arena with a brilliant and bitter pamphlet against the Emperor and his regime, *De l'esprit de Conquête et de l'Usurpation*. After launching unsuccessful negotiations and intrigues in favour of Count Bernadotte's candidacy to the French throne, he returned to Paris in 1814.

In the France of the Restoration, always exposed to the danger of reactionary absolutism, he became widely known as a defender and theorist of constitutional monarchy, and soon one of those disconcerting episodes which characterize his life was to make him even more famous. When Napoleon left Elba in 1815 and landed in southern France, Constant naturally feared and opposed the usurper's return, and his love for Madame Récamier, who was a royalist, fanned his anti-Napoleonic zeal. Supposedly it was his desire to outdo his rival Forbin, who had impressed Madame Récamier with heroic words and gestures, that induced Constant to publish a wildly anti-Napoleonic article in the *Journal des Débats* of 19 March, which was on the very eve of the King's flight from Paris! One grandiloquent passage of this manifesto has acquired ironic fame: "I will not go, a miserable renegade, dragging myself from one power to another, covering infamy by sophisms and stammering profane words to redeem a shameful life."[1] Constant fled shortly before Napoleon's arrival in the capital, but when he saw that the whole country was rapidly joining the Emperor, he returned to Paris, resigned and prepared for the worst. The unexpected happened: Napoleon realized that he had to pursue a liberal policy, and instead of persecuting Constant he turned to him for advice! Constant responded to these overtures and on 22 April, only a month after his heroic article, joined the imperial Council of State. More important, he became the chief author of Napoleon's new liberal constitution, the so-called "Additional Act to the Constitutions of the Empire", popularly known as "le Benjamin". His commentary on this document, entitled *Principes de politique*, has become one of his most important works on political theory.

A few years later Constant published his *Mémoires sur les Cent-Jours*. Despite its apologetic purpose, this book, with its lucid analysis of the events and their causes, is a significant historical document. The accounts of the conversations with Napoleon have literary value and give an insight into the Emperor's character. The apology is undeniably clever: Constant points out that it was the intransigence of his opponents,

[1] Quoted this way in Elizabeth W. Schermerhorn, *Benjamin Constant* (Boston & New York, 1924), p. 273.

78

the reactionary advocates of royal absolutism, which had made the country ready to hail Napoleon's return. He even insinuates that they may have favoured the King's flight in the hope of re-establishing despotism more easily after his second restoration. In any case this flight changed the whole question, for the invasion of France by the allied powers became inevitable and it was the true patriot's duty to support the only defender of the French soil: ". . . I have been blamed because I did not die for the throne I had defended on the 19th of March. But on the 20th I raised my eyes, I saw that the throne had disappeared and that France remained."[2] Besides, the Emperor was serious in his desire to establish a liberal regime, and it was incumbent on Constant and other liberals to aid him in his efforts and to protect his good intentions against his autocratic instincts. These arguments are plausible and at least partly justified. In vain! The ambiguity of Constant's actions could not be reasoned away. Many people refused to believe in the good faith of a man who changed his allegiance so rapidly, and his professions of patriotism seemed exaggerated to those who remembered his return to Paris with the allied armies in 1814. His name became the object of

[2] Benjamin Constant, *Mémoires sur les Cent-Jours* (Paris, 1829), p. 117.

obvious puns, and all his later prestige and his proofs of courage could not entirely efface the memory of that fatal article in the *Journal des Débats*. Constant had a genius for doing the wrong thing at the wrong time.

Through a memorial of justification to the King, Constant escaped reprisals after the second Restoration. Yet he considered it safer to spend some months in England with his wife. In September 1816 he returned to France, and until his death most of his energies were devoted to political life. At first he sympathized with the "Doctrinaires", a centrist group, but soon he moved more to the left and became one of the leaders of the liberal opposition—together with men like Manuel, Foy, Lafayette, and Sébastiani. In this quality, Constant played a leading part in the development of modern parliamentary government. He was a member of parliament during most of the Restoration period, representing successively the Sarthe, Paris, and the Lower Rhine (Alsace). His opponents feared the implacable logic and pungency of his speeches, and the invalid representative (ever since an accident in 1818 he walked with a crutch) was a familiar figure in Paris. In numerous articles and pamphlets, which found a public throughout Europe, he tried to instruct his country in the processes of constitutional government. His model was England and he was probably France's foremost authority on English conditions. Whenever there was any violation of freedom or legality, the "knight errant of liberalism" took up the challenge. Notably his essays and speeches in defence of the freedom of publication are instructive even now. Constant also took an active interest in such typical liberalist questions as the extension of the jury system, the condemnation of slavery, the defence of secular education against ecclesiastical encroachments, and the protection of Protestants against discrimination. The chief source for the study of his ideas on constitutionalism is the *Cours de politique constitutionnelle*, published 1818–19, a collection of most of his previous political writings.

Constant lived to see the revolution of July 1830, which put a definitive end to Bourbon rule. He played a leading part in the elevation of the Duke of Orléans to the throne, and became an important member of the new King's Council of State. Again there were circumstances which have been considered incriminating: Constant was still addicted to gambling, and King Louis-Philippe paid his debts. This fact harmed Constant in public opinion, although he did not become Louis-Philippe's creature and continued to defend his own independent convictions. At the end of 1830 he died, and the last weeks of his life were embittered by his failure to be elected to the French Academy. But his funeral on 12 December became an apotheosis and a political demonstration. All Paris was in the streets when Constant's body was borne in state to the Père Lachaise cemetery, and the event has found an echo in the letters and diaries of many contemporaries.

The Nature of Constant's Liberalism

Constant's apparent political instability conceals a deep, unswerving consistency. It was rather his time which was unstable: regimes came and went, and political life was in continual flux. Constant's loyalty was never attached to any one particular regime or form of government but always to the principle of individual liberty, and to realize and defend this ideal he was prepared to experiment.

This is not the place to give a complete account of Constant's political doctrine or to trace the stages of its development. What concerns us here is the essential *nature* of his liberalism, the philosophy which underlies his political thinking and is implicit in all his writings on politics.

A recurrent theme in Constant's political works is his strong, and sometimes violent, critique of Rousseau's theories in the *Contrat social*. This is all the more noteworthy because the *Contrat social* is the logical continuation of the "Second Discourse", which so profoundly influenced Constant. In fact the discovery, in the "Second Discourse", that man is essentially divided within himself, that there is a fragmentation at the very core of his being, is not original with Rousseau. Religious thinkers had grappled with this problem, and Pascal's apology of Christianity in the *Pensées* largely hinges on the contention that this ontological dilemma can only be explained by the doctrine of original sin. But Rousseau, as we have seen, offers another explanation, and one of infinite consequence: man has *lost himself* by living exclusively by the opinion of the "others", his nature has been perverted and emptied of its substance through his existence in the sham world of society, so that his present condition is the result of a long process of self-estrangement. By thus analyzing the whole problem in terms of alienation, Rousseau shifts it from the religious-theological to the socio-political domain. He thereby formulates the crucial premise of all revolutionary thought, for it is only one step to the conclusion that the basic dilemma of human existence can be solved on the political level—that man can be changed by political action. Rousseau himself takes this final step with perfect consistency: the *Contrat social* is his attempt at just such a solution.

Man has changed far too much to return to his original (and, incidentally, purely hypothetical) state of nature. He has become a social being, living in political association. What he can do is to transform this manner of existence, founded on inequality and arbitrary power, into a *legitimate* situation. Legally, even if not historically, all social and political association is based on a social contract in which men have abandoned an essential part of their individualities and "alienated" on behalf of the "general will"; this "general will" is the only legitimate source of political authority.

We cannot go into the practical conclusions which Rousseau draws from his theory. What interests us is the fact that he converts the fatal and involuntary self-estrangement of civilized man, diagnosed in the "Second Discourse", into a *voluntary* alienation in the social contract. This alienation is *absolute*, for the "general will" is much more to Rousseau than a mere legal concept, denoting the opinion of the majority: it marks the *creative* convergence of the previously isolated individual wills, their synthesis into a true community, and is nothing less than the embodiment of an ideal human nature. In this way, social and political association becomes a positive enterprise of education, it *cures* man's decadent nature by raising him on to a superior level of

84

being. When the individual obeys the general will, expressed in the law, in fact he obeys his own higher will. Anarchic individual liberty is thus elevated to voluntary constraint, pristine independence is replaced by purposeful moral action, and man is ennobled by his transformation into a citizen.

Constant does accept Rousseau's principle that the general will is the legitimate source of sovereignty. But while for Rousseau sovereignty is by its very nature indivisible and absolute, Constant would limit and divide it in every conceivable way. He sharply attacks the theorist of the *Contrat social* who "cherished all theories of liberty and furnished pretexts for all pretensions to tyranny".[3] The chief target for his criticism is that total alienation of the individual to the general will which is the point of departure of what he terms "the eternal metaphysics of the *Contrat social*".[4] The French Revolution has shown that in practice the general will to which we submit may be far from representing our ideal selves: we simply submit to those men who wield the power. Instead of attaining to a superior form of freedom, the individual is crushed under the onslaught of state and society.

[3] P. 1215, in the *Principes de politique*.
[4] P. 1216, in the *Principes*.

However, a purely empirical critique is not sufficient. Constant himself, after all, is all too conscious of the dilemma which Rousseau's doctrine is meant to solve: the corruption and fragmentation of modern man. His critique cuts much deeper and goes to the very root of Rousseau's brilliant and dangerous construction: the ideal of the ancient Greek *polis*, where life seemed to have a *completeness* unknown to us and where man's personal existence found its fulfilment in his subjection to the State and in his devotion to the public good. Constant tries to show that this form of existence is an anachronism. The ancient concept of freedom was collective, so he argues, but ours can only be individual. The citizen of a small Greek city state could sacrifice his private independence in exchange for a concrete participation in collective power, but now, in the era of huge states governed by representation, such participation is almost nil. Moreover, the means of individual happiness have increased, so that our sacrifice would be immeasurably greater. But Constant also advances a more basic argument: the ancients, who were "in the youth of moral life", were still capable of complete convictions, for they had that enthusiasm which enables men to devote themselves entirely to a cause. Modern man, however, is weighed down by experience and is incapable of undivided enthusiasm, for he observes himself incessantly and fears the appearance of ridicule. Thus he is devoid of moral strength and all his convictions are weak, floating, and incomplete.[5] Constant understands and shares the modern nostalgia for the vitality of the ancient republics: "The old elements of a nature anterior to ours, as it were, seem to awaken in us with these memories."[6] But modern man is so degenerate that he cannot recover this unbroken, integral existence. Again we find the familiar contrast between Greek simplicity and modern dividedness, derived from German aesthetic theory. In the thinking of Schiller and Friedrich Schlegel this concept had remained largely (though not entirely) confined to the realm of aesthetics, but let us mention in passing that even in its specific application to political theory Constant had a precursor: his ideas on this point resemble those of the young Wilhelm von Humboldt, another theorist from Schiller's sphere.[7]

We see the theoretical consistency of Constant's

[5] Cf. p. 1047, in the *Esprit de Conquête*.

[6] Pp. 1027–8, in the *Esprit de Conquête*.

[7] Cf. Wilhelm von Humboldt's essay "Ideen zu einem Versuch, die Grenzen der Wirksamkeit des Staats zu bestimmen". Although this essay was written in 1792, it appeared only much later. Yet Constant *may* have been familiar with the gist of Humboldt's ideas, for they were common knowledge in some of the circles in which he moved in Germany.

anti-Rousseauistic critique. He not only understands, but accepts Rousseau's diagnosis of the
modern malady and agrees with his analysis of its
causes, but from this revolutionary premise he
draws a diametrically opposite, a determinedly
non-revolutionary conclusion. Rousseau had
hoped to restore the lost unity of human nature
by welding together the individual and society,
the private and the public sphere. But Constant
believes that precisely owing to the extreme
weakness and corruption of modern man, this
subtle dialectical synthesis is as illusory as a return to the "naïveté" and objectivity of ancient
literature. If the social contract were absolute,
man's social existence would entirely supplant
and dissolve his individual essence. The "citizen", far from being a higher type of man, would
merely be a soulless mirror of public opinion and
an instrument of political power, devoid of all
human value. Therefore, as against Rousseau's
nostalgic monism, Constant defends an extreme
and conscious dualism. The individual should be
protected against the community rather than
assimilated by it. The dividedness of modern
man, which cannot be artificially repaired,
should be reflected in the duality of the political
structure, in the strict separation between the
private and the public sphere. This fundamental principle of liberalism is the political

parallel of Constant's version of romantic individualism—the subject's self-affirmation against
objective reality. The separation of the spheres is
formulated in the declaration of the inalienable
rights of man, which in effect separates the man
from the citizen by circumscribing a private
domain on which no society or government can
infringe. These rights are inalienable because
they are derived from man's moral and intellectual autonomy, i.e. from his very humanity. The
declaration of rights, in other words, is nothing
less than a legal delineation and definition of
human nature. For Constant, then, the individual's alienation in the social contract is only
partial. The "general will" is not a moral and
metaphysical entity, embodying man's ideal
nature, but a purely formal principle of legality,
implicating a strictly limited part of man.

But Constant upholds still another principle
of separation which is characteristic of early
liberalism: the distinction between "active" and
"passive" citizenship, which had first appeared in
the electoral laws of the revolutionary period and
especially in the "Idéologue" constitution of the
year III. Civil rights are to be granted to every-
one, but political rights (voting and holding
office) should be confined to the owners of
property.

For Constant, as for all early bourgeois liberals,

the question of property is of central importance. On one decisive point, however, he deviates sharply from the prevailing view. Most of these liberals follow the Lockean tradition according to which property is one, and perhaps the most important, of the *natural* rights of man. Constant insists that property is a creation of society. "Property is not anterior to society," he writes in a strikingly Rousseauistic argument, "for without the association that guarantees it, it would be nothing but the right of the first occupant, in other words the law of the strongest, and therefore a right which is not a right."[8] A significant approach, considering that this was one of the crucial points of difference between the Jacobins of the Terror and the moderate middle-class Girondins—between Robespierre and Condorcet. The moderate Constant in effect adopts Robespierre's point of view! But again, as with the problem of sovereignty, Constant draws opposite conclusions from his Rousseauistic premises. Having established that property is only a social convention and thus theoretically subject to social legislation, he does his best to prove that it is nevertheless as inalienable as the truly natural rights such as personal freedom, freedom of religion and freedom of opinion. He treats the possible abolition of private property

[8] Pp. 1200–01, in the *Principes*.

as a chimerical scheme in the heads of some un-
realistic philosophers. We need the institution of
property for our collective subsistence, for its
disappearance would destroy the division of
labour, which is essential to the progress of the
arts and sciences. Moreover, legal violations of
property interests would tend to multiply and in-
vite resistance and conflict, so that the ultimate
consequence would be infringements on the
natural rights. But could not the same thing be
said about *any* act which runs counter to any individual interest? Constant's pleas for the in-
violability of property show a certain uneasiness,
a peculiar lack of certainty, and indeed their
theoretical weakness is evident. His purely prag-
matic, conventional reasons cannot raise property
to the rank of such fundamental rights as personal freedom, which are derived from human
nature. Constant's attempt to unite Rousseauism
with a more moderate tradition is not very successful here.

Political rights should be reserved for those
who have an independent income, for the man
who must work for a living has neither the intellectual detachment that would enable him to
vote with true enlightenment nor the factual independence that would allow him to vote according to his conscience. This reasoning, not very
original as such, takes on special significance in

the light of Constant's philosophical premises. When he is caught in the relentless process of production and in the web of material dependence, man in fact *has* no private sphere, and loses the freedom and independence which are his by definition and by right. No doubt Constant had more than an inkling of this particular form of alienation, which was to assume such alarming dimensions as the nineteenth century ground on. He realized that the declaration of human rights tends to be a mere legal fiction. Only the possession of property can translate this fiction into reality. Supreme and frightening irony! In modern society, only property, itself a social institution, can bring man back to himself and restore a semblance of that intelligent insight and moral autonomy which is supposedly an inalienable attribute of human nature!

In this perspective, property is not merely the historical weapon of one particular class: for Constant, as for other nineteenth-century liberals, it has the scope of a universal principle. Yet he is far from their dynamic optimism and even farther from that economic "survival of the fittest" mentality, that shameless cult of self-enrichment, which was taking shape during his lifetime. In many ways his relation to property is aristocratic (or perhaps patrician) rather than bourgeois. In the *Esprit de Conquête* he affirms the superiority of established fortunes as against the mentality of the newly rich. In the *Principes* he limits political rights to the landowners, excluding those citizens whose property is wholly "industrial". Later he reversed himself on this point, since he had to fight those reactionary interests of the Restoration period that tried to hamper the freedom of commerce and industrial development. Yet his earlier views, influenced by Physiocratic theories and by the example of the English landed gentry, prove that he did not whole-heartedly welcome the coming industrial revolution. Landed property, so he writes in the *Principes*, engenders a prudently progressive state of mind, for the cultivator is dependent on nature and not on men, which makes him regular in his habits and enlightened in his judgments. Industrial property, on the other hand, advances by leaps and bounds and is largely subject to chance, since it depends on the rich and their vanity, pride, and luxury. Its only goal is profit, an abstract and purely quantitative value, so that this type of property cannot improve, but merely increase. It tends to create a personality without stability, without a sense of intrinsic value, the plaything of an increasingly rootless society. Constant later found an argument in favour of commerce and "industrial property": *credit* is a strong weapon against all encroachments on liberty. Rampart of individual freedom or guarantee of stability—property, for Constant, is always a protective device. It is not dynamic but static, not an instrument of indefinite social progress but a principle of security, affording an aristocratic sanctuary against the onrush of despotism and of a growing mass civilization.

Therefore Constant is extremely sceptical with regard to the profit motive, that idol of a rising bourgeoisie. The prevalent liberal attitude was expressed by Bentham, whose works had influenced Madame de Staël and some of Constant's Idéologue friends: Bentham believed that self-interest ("enlightened", of course) could play the same role in modern society as "virtue" in the republics of antiquity. In order to appreciate the distance which separates Constant from such a view, we must turn to his book *De l'esprit de Conquête et de l'Usurpation*, the most remarkable of his political writings from our present-day point of view. This brief work of 1813 is much more than an anti-Napoleonic tract. With rare penetration Constant analyzes certain ominous developments of French society under Napoleon, but he does not stop there: pushing these trends to their conclusion, he arrives at a prophetic prognosis of some of the most negative aspects of modern life.

The second part of the book, which deals with

usurpation, is less noteworthy than the first. It owes much to Montesquieu's remarks on despotism, which Constant combines with his observations on Bonaparte's France. Yet he draws a vivid though somewhat polemical picture of this first modern dictatorship, with its flagging intellectual life, its hypocrisy, and its insecurity. There is a note of optimism, justified after the debacle of 1812: since it is an anachronism, this state of affairs cannot possibly last.

The section on the "spirit of conquest" has wider scope. It begins with a critical examination of the morality of heroism as applied to modern times. Constant makes it clear that he does not absolutely condemn the quest for warlike glory, which is a perfectly appropriate way of life in certain periods. Thus the spirit of heroism was suited to the world of the ancient Greek city states, but no longer corresponds to the realities of contemporary life. Once more the opposition between ancients and moderns! War has ceased to be useful and the quest of military glory is not an authentic component of the modern personality. We live in an enlightened world of universal commerce and desire the peaceful enjoyment of our growing luxury. Yet Constant is far removed from the Enlightenment optimism which, on the surface, seems to inspire such statements. He is by no means confident that militarism will disappear all by itself. The spirit of war may be an anachronism but it can be artificially created, for modern man is weak and infinitely malleable. The result will be a frightening combination of savagery and falsity, a new kind of barbarism, all the more atrocious as it is strengthened by the effeminacy of luxurious living and by a sordidly materialistic view of life. Does Constant have a presentiment of the unholy alliance between industrialism and militarism? A new caste of warriors may arise, more ferocious than any preceding military class. Those men will profess a morality of exalted self-sacrifice and noble self-transcendence, but their true motive will be squalid self-interest. Therefore, if self-interest has taken the place of ancient "virtue", it is merely another sign of modern man's corruption.

Once it is established, the system of conquest will be self-perpetuating, but it must be sustained by lies and propaganda since it is out of tune with the spirit of the times. The government cannot admit its real aim, which is nothing less than the conquest of the world: ". . . it would speak of national independence, rounding off frontiers, commercial interests, precautions dictated by foresight, and who knows what else?— for the vocabulary of hypocrisy and injustice is inexhaustible".[9] The aggressive nationalism of the State will negate the very existence of other nations. Even in domestic life an inhuman atmosphere of suspicion will prevail: wives will spy on their husbands, children on their parents. Meanwhile the regimentation of youth will lead to a general growth of ignorance. Few authors have been so clearly aware of the dangers of uniformity: "Above all, uniformity is the great word nowadays. It is a pity that one cannot pull down the towns to rebuild them all on an identical plan, level the mountains, so that the ground may be the same everywhere: and I am surprised that the inhabitants have not all been ordered to wear the same costume, so that the master may no longer encounter any irregular mixture and any shocking variety."[10] Paradoxically, this atrocious desire for a grotesque symmetry has sprung from a revolution which took place in the name of human rights and freedom. And as he faces the spectre of this levelling process, Constant, the lifelong liberal and relentless opponent of the Ancien Régime, suddenly speaks almost like a traditionalist. He fears revolutions, for they usually miss their mark by overstepping it, and is horrified by the growth of abstractness in modern life, by the impersonality of the centralized mammoth state. Therefore he

[9] P. 1004. [10] P. 1014.

favours administrative decentralization, would fortify the local spirit, and expresses respect for established customs and veneration for the past. Reformers should cautiously modify traditional institutions, for if such institutions do not actually clash with justice they are always preferable to logical constructions that may be "metaphysically" perfect, but have no deeper human roots.

Such statements give the full measure of Constant's pessimism. How could a man with his tragic insight have confidence in the "constructive" dynamism of the profit motive? It is not surprising that he was also unimpressed by the principle of the greatest happiness for the greatest number, that utilitarian precept of morality which Bentham had derived from Hellvétius and which proved so attractive to contemporary liberals. Here lies the core of the difference between Constant and the eighteenth-century "philosophical" tradition. For the *philosophes* the purpose of political association is the promotion of human happiness, and their ideal is the welfare state. Constant is basically untouched by the prevailing eudaemonism, though he does occasionally use its vocabulary, which is the vocabulary of his period. What interests him is not welfare, but legitimacy.

Influenced by Montesquieu's *Esprit des Lois*

and by the practice of English parliamentarianism, Constant advocates the division of powers and an elaborate system of checks and balances. He does not, like Montesquieu, distinguish merely three strictly separate powers, but five: the King, the executive, the "representative power of duration" (upper house), the "representative power of opinion" (lower house), and the judiciary. The power of the King is neutral and has the task of keeping the other four in proper balance: Constant, probably the most important theorist of constitutional monarchy in early nineteenth-century France, was one of the first who consistently defended the principle that "the King reigns, but does not govern". He clearly seeks a balance between the conservative and the progressive forces, the static and the dynamic elements. His object is to create institutions that are both strong and flexible enough to lead the forces of dynamic change into legal channels.

The personal accent of Constant's liberalism lies in his painstaking adherence to all legal and constitutional *forms*, which he describes as "the tutelary divinities of human associations".[11] These forms have intrinsic value, and their slightest violation ("*l'arbitraire*") is fatal, for it

[11] Quoted in Georges de Lauris, *Benjamin Constant et les idées libérales* (Paris, 1904), p. 235.

entails further violations and undermines the very principle of legality. Therefore all ministers who direct arbitrary acts are to be treated as criminals of civil law. More than that: even those men who execute their orders are to be held personally responsible. No one can claim that he acted under duress, and fear is no excuse: "Man can never totally lose his faculty of judgment and reject the intelligence which nature has given him for his conduct. No profession can dispense him of using it."[12] Again we touch the sensitive core of Constant's thought: through blind obedience man renounces his very humanity. He who takes orders without questioning has *factually* been transformed into an "instrument", a mere object. Such are the eternal creatures of despotism whom Constant violently stigmatizes: "Woe to those zealous and docile instruments who want to make us believe that they are eternally oppressed —indefatigable agents of all existing tyrannies, posthumous enemies of all overthrown tyrannies."[13] They always serve him who is in power, only to turn against him after his fall, for they are chameleons that adapt their colour to their surroundings—mere empty shells, devoid of all moral substance and *moulded* by the conditions

[12] Quoted in Georges de Lauris, *Benjamin Constant et les idées libérales* (Paris, 1904), p. 254.
[13] P. 1110, in the *Principes*.

which happen to prevail. In fact they have already reached that zero point which Constant's pessimism foresees and fears: man's essence has been dissolved, man's nature crushed. But are these men fully responsible for their actions? Constant's answer is the categorical statement that they are: the law cannot and should not assume that man is not a free and intelligent agent.

The varied elements of Constant's political thought, his vacillations on the question of property, the aristocratic components of his liberalism—these are factors which have led to the view that Constant, as a political thinker, marks the transition between the eighteenth and the nineteenth century. Without being false, this perspective is limited and fails to bring out the inner consistency of his thought. It has been said that Constant is still very much (too much) a man of the eighteenth century, since he attaches exaggerated value to general definitions and abstract principles. This type of criticism comes from the later nineteenth century, at times too triumphant about its pet discovery: the principle of historical relativity. But Constant's definitions, his principles of government, the legal forms on which he places such emphasis— they are not comparable to the general truths by which a certain eighteenth-century tradition wished to reconstruct reality according to universal reason and common sense. They are principles of legality, purely protective and defensive, desperate attempts to exorcise and master the chaotic flux of events by means of reason.

Constant knew much about the tragic cruelty of history. We may compare him to a coastal dweller, engaged in building dykes against the on-rushing waves. He had a nightmarish vision of the future and recognized the forces which had been let loose. The *Esprit de Conquête* is one of the first penetrating cultural diagnoses of a very pessimistic and very lucid nineteenth-century tradition and its author deserves to be named as a precursor of such theorists as Burckhardt and Tocqueville.

V

CONSTANT AND RELIGION

In its original conception, the study on religion which Constant set out to write at the age of eighteen and on which he worked intermittently for the rest of his life was to be a treatise on the history of polytheism, more or less in the eighteenth-century tradition. But his work developed with him, was continually modified, and steadily increased in scope until it grew into a universal comparative history of religion. The first volume of *De la religion considérée dans sa source, sa forme et ses développements* appeared in 1824; four additional volumes followed during Constant's lifetime, and two more, entitled *Du polythéisme romain*, were published posthumously, but the study has remained unfinished.

Constant's erudition was extraordinary. He was familiar with all important eighteenth-century and Idéologue studies on his subject, with the work of Adam Ferguson, and with the German theories, notably of Creuzer and Herder. Constant was one of the early representatives of the new ideal of exact scholarship. This applies even to his working method, for he worked with an elaborate system of files, which was a rare procedure in his time. He was very anxious to avoid the generalizing constructions in which the eighteenth-century theorists indulged all too easily, and through the meticulous study and analysis of a large body of facts which he had accumulated, he hoped to discover the laws that govern the evolution of religious forms. However, the data at his disposal were limited, for the science of religion was still in its infancy, and Constant's work, although it has played an honourable and even pioneering role in the development of this science, is now antiquated in most respects. Perhaps many of his ideas have not yet been sufficiently studied, but this is hardly the place for such a study, nor even for a detailed account of Constant's theories. What interests us is the meaning and significance of religion in his own personal philosophy of life.

The eighteenth-century tradition, at least in France, had always reduced the fact of religion to something extraneous to the religious experience, such as ignorance, fear, astrolatry, or priestly authority. Constant, however, finds the source of religion in the *religious feeling*, which he defines as a natural fact, an original and universal component of human nature. But this feeling is subjective and vague: in order to acquire content, coherence, and reality it must be communicated to others and needs their approval. Thus it becomes "objectivized" in "religious forms" and participates in the development of society, in the process of historical change. This is not a smooth process. The external structure is originally a genuine reflection of the feeling which underlies it, but soon the forms threaten to become dead weights which stifle the authentic experience, for all social institutions tend to be self-perpetuating even after they have outlived their usefulness. Whenever the religious institutions have become empty vestiges of the past, allied with reactionary political interests, there arise the mutually related phenomena of superstition and freethinking. Superstition is the perversion of religiousness, the product of a formalism without content. Freethinking and atheism react against this formalism and have a useful destructive function as long as antiquated forms are sustained by political oppression. But with the advent of religious freedom, atheism becomes an unnatural and objectionable attitude. In Constant's perspective, the anti-religious propaganda of the *philosophes* is a passing stage which precedes and prepares a revival of true religiousness. He believes that the time for such a revival has come and that "freedom" is the password in religion as in politics. A true Protestant in the original sense of the word, he exalts the "free religions" as against the "sacerdotal religions". In the former the individual religious conscience, which is now highly developed and articulate, is no longer hampered and weighed down by an over-size ecclesiastical structure. Religiousness as an authentic, essential experience which is in danger of estrangement: we recognize Constant's eternal preoccupation. This time, however, there is a distinct note of optimism, for in the domain of religion the relentless process of alienation seems to be reversed. In the course of the historical development of religious forms, from "fetish-ism" (= animism) via polytheism to monotheism, religiousness is gradually purified. There are in-dications that its final and perfect form, for Con-stant, is an emotional type of Christianity which expresses the genuine spirit of the Gospel.

Constant's style becomes almost poetic when he describes the religious feeling, which is an in-stinctive knowledge of a realm that transcends the mechanism of everyday life, an obscure nostalgia for higher things. The individual feels that he is not isolated, but is in communion with the in-finite and has access to the hidden forces of the universe. In one important respect, the religious feeling runs counter to all other human impulses: it is not self-directed, but disinterested to the

point of sacrifice. We already know Constant's
aversion to ethical utilitarianism and eudaemonism. In fact, the preface of *De la religion* contains a
sharp polemic against the morality of "enlightened self-interest" with its ideal of "happiness".
At best, this morality can do away with human
vice, but at the same time it proscribes all
generous emotions such as pity, sympathy and
selflessness. The depressingly drab, almost suf-
focating atmosphere of d'Holbach's *Système de la
nature* expresses the quintessence of this dry and
ungenerous aspect of eighteenth-century thought.
The practical result of this spirit has been the
abject servility which typified the imperial era.
Political freedom can only be established and
maintained by sacrifice, and therefore requires a
morality which is based on self-denial and seeks
human perfection rather than individual well-
being. Moreover, "generosity" and "enthusiasm" are intrinsic values and fundamental human
qualities which man cannot discard without per-
verting his nature. Let us recall Constant's
admiration for the heroic spirit of the Greek city
states, and his pessimistic conviction that heroism is impossible because of the incurable degeneration of modern man. Now it appears that
through the religious experience man is still
capable of the spirit of sacrifice. The definition of
religious feeling merges with that of sincerity:

when the individual breaks through the factitious crust of his superficial ego and descends to the core of his being, he finds the urge for self-transcendence. In this way individualism is overcome from the inside, as it were, for self-abnegation is the highest affirmation of personality. André Gide, who resembles Constant in more than one respect, enunciates a similar conception of religiousness and formulates it in the evangelical paradox: "For whosoever will save his life shall lose it; but whosoever will lose his life . . ., the same shall save it."

By penetrating to his religious essence, man overcomes not only his self-estrangement but also his isolation from the world and from his fellow men. The idea of man's inherent religiousness seems to solve many things—so many, in fact, that we are entitled to ask ourselves whether Constant's desire for a revival of religion, so symptomatic of his time, springs from an authentically religious spirit and conviction. To what degree is his own religiosity a projection of purely emotional rather than truly religious needs, and a handy hypothesis that may solve certain awkward problems? When we look at his life and consult his journals, we find that he is particularly attracted by the comfort that religion may afford in hours of adversity and suffering. Thus Constant, who was obsessed with the fear of death, could never understand how his friend Julie Thalma was able to reject religious consolation even on her deathbed. Religion can also offer an escape from life's worries, and in 1807, at the most tempestuous and upsetting period of his relationship with Madame de Staël, Constant toyed with the idea of mysticism. Under the influence of his cousin De Langallerie, who belonged to a sect of Quietists, he longed to renounce all volition and intellection, passively opening up his soul to God, who was to take care of all anguishing problems and decisions. The temptation of escapism is all too obvious: there was in Constant, as in Gide, a strong desire to lose himself. In the Paris of the early Restoration years, at the house of Madame Récamier, Constant took part in spiritualist séances which were conducted by Madame de Krüdner, a sort of fashionable religious practitioner. Madame de Krüdner promised Constant to establish a "soul-bond" between him and Madame Récamier. On both occasions Constant's "mysticism" was not only unauthentic, but very shortlived: his natural scepticism could not be subdued.

Indeed Constant acts like a man who tries to escape recognising that he is unable to believe. This does not mean, of course, that he is indifferent to religious problems. Such problems deeply concern him, but when he is confronted with them he tends to evade the issue. His arguments in favour of the existence of God and the immortality of the soul can in effect be reduced to the statement: why should not these things be true, since we are naturally inclined to believe them? Constant condemns atheism for its lack of feeling, its emotionally sterile atmosphere, much more than for its rejection of religious truth: even here the accent lies on the subjective experience rather than on the objective content. Avoiding the problem of religious faith by trying to take it for granted, Constant dissolves religion into a vague emotional attitude. This subjectivization of religion is typical of the early nineteenth century.

VI

CONSTANT AND MODERNITY

Benjamin Constant, though one of the first intellects of his time, was not really great, and yet he is more living now than most of his contemporaries. In fact, it is the timeliness of Constant, his *modernity*, which is his most striking characteristic. Not only did his thought, with great intensity, revolve about certain specifically modern problems, but he was one of the first in France who realized that the fact of being a "modern" is a problem in itself.

Constant verbalized some of the primary themes which were to run through nineteenth-century thought—preoccupations that are with us even now. He clearly saw and felt the rift between man and the universe and between the individual and society, and he knew that man was alienated from himself. Constant understood the temptation of solving this dilemma on the socio-political plane, but he rejected it. Throughout the nineteenth century the anti-liberal critique, faithful to a monistic conception, attacked the separation between the private and the public sphere as an institutionalized fragmentation of human nature. Constant's liberalism, defensive as it is, can at least oppose a cogent argument to this pungent criticism. The truth is, Constant has no cure for the dividedness of modern man, neither a political nor, like Schiller, an aesthetic one: his nostalgic religious solution is singularly unconvincing. But the very insight into the problem, and its clear formulation, is no mediocre achievement.

Even Constant's self-exploration should be placed in this wider context, for it is much more than the narcissism of a mere egomaniac. If Constant grappled with the problem of "sincerity", it was also because he felt that nothing was certain any more, and that man himself had become questionable. What indeed is man's essence? Can it be seized by a descent into the subjectivity of feeling, or on the contrary fixed in "objective" mathematical formulae? Or can it be circumscribed and rescued by legal definitions, such as the declaration of the "inalienable rights" of man? What Constant faced was nothing less than the spectre of *dehumanization*.

Constant's modernity is not confined to his ideas, but extends to his own life and personality. Even his internationalism foreshadows a peculiarly modern type of uprootedness, and his incurable gambling mania is a symbol of the same adventurous restlessness. In spite of a recurrent desire for security, he is magically attracted by the vicissitudes of chance, for they express his basic experience of reality. It is the experience of a man for whom all social and metaphysical values and certainties have begun to disintegrate and who no longer feels, so to speak, that he is firmly rooted in the universe. The numerous paradoxes and contradictions of Constant's life make him the perfect model of his own theory of the modern personality. This correspondence between life and thought goes so far that he actually *lives* the French–German polarization which is one of his recurrent ideas. He is continually torn between the worldly brilliance of the Parisian *salons* and the studious solitude of the German libraries, and alternates between the political and social upheavals of France and the paternalistic smugness of the small German states. Constant is almost the prototype of "interesting individuality" as defined by Friedrich Schlegel, a fact which the critic should bring out but keep in a proper perspective. Friedrich Schlegel said that modern literature prefers effect to harmony, and seeks only the unusual. Perhaps his concept of the "interesting" should be applied to criticism as well, and it may be worth while to examine the whole biographical tradition of nineteenth-century criticism in this light. Is this tradition always motivated by the desire to "explain" a writer's work by studying his life, or is it partly due to an indiscreet and digging interest in everything individual, striking, and piquant? If literary criticism is too exclusively concerned with the consideration of a writer's individuality, it prepares and furthers that exhibitionism, that empty and inflated sensationalism which is one of the blights of our time. Traditional Constant criticism, dominated ever since Sainte-Beuve by a one-sidedly biographical and anecdotal approach, cannot be completely absolved from this reproach.

At first sight Constant's lifelong enterprise of exact scholarship seems paradoxical in a man of his character and temperament. Perhaps he felt that *facts*, ascertained and interpreted by scholarly methods, are solid and indubitable, fixed points in the unseizable flux of change. We know that through his work on religion Constant wanted to "leave a trace" in the world (as Berger puts it in Malraux's *Noyers de l'Altenbourg*), a trace that could not be effaced by time. He was only half-successful: not only are scholarly works subject to ageing, but Constant's study is not completed. His entire life has this unfinished quality, and bears the characteristic stamp of "halfness" and near-success. The word "almost" could describe him: he almost finished the *Cahier rouge* and *Cécile*, he almost became a minister, he almost entered the French Academy and he was almost religious—in fact he was almost a great man. There is something ill-defined and indefinable about Constant. His talents, activities, and interests are varied and numerous, but they remain fragmentary and are never synthesized into a harmonious or even an entirely coherent *whole*. Constant's astonishing versatility is at the opposite pole from Goethean universality.

Although Constant is not Adolphe, nor even the hero of *Cécile* or the *Cahier rouge*, it is extremely difficult to keep him apart from his protagonists. This is not merely because he endowed his heroes with many of his own characteristics: perhaps they influenced him in their turn, so that he came to resemble them. And it is possible that Constant consciously or unconsciously acted out his own theory of the modern personality? This question is obviously unanswerable, but is not the very fact that it can be asked almost a confirmation of the theory? The world which Constant both describes and represents is one where nothing is fixed and indubitable and where being and seeming, truth and make-believe are inextricably intermingled and often indistinguishable. Who is to say what is fake and what is "genuine", and who can draw the line between originality and imitation? The *actor* is the modern type *par excellence*. Friedrich Nietzsche's polemic against Richard Wagner, which constitutes the most searching and profound critique of modernity, is essentially an analysis of the actor.

Is Benjamin Constant an unauthentic "individual"? We probably must answer yes, only to add that this judgment is of limited scope and beside the point. Constant's real "authenticity" lies in his urge to understand and clarify problems, and in the inner consistency of his thought. He never overcame his fragmentation, but though the completeness and integration which he sought was denied him in his life, he realized it in literature in the perfect articulation of the world of *Adolphe*, where everything seems translucent to reason.

BIOGRAPHICAL TABLE

1767
: 25 October: birth of Constant in Lausanne. 10 November: death of his mother.

1774–82
: Succession of private tutors. Peregrinations between Brussels, Lausanne, and Holland. Stay of two months in London and Oxford (1780).

1782–3
: Student at the University of Erlangen.

1783–5
: Student in Edinburgh.

1785–6
: Paris, Brussels, Lausanne. Liaison with Madame Johannot in Brussels. Love for Mrs. Trevor in Lausanne.

1786–7
: Second stay in Paris. Meets Madame de Charrière.

1787
: English escapade (June–October), Holland, Switzerland.

1788–94
: Stay at the court of Brunswick (interrupted by many travels, mostly to Switzerland).

1789	Marriage with Wilhelmine von Cramm.
1793	Liaison with Charlotte von Marenholz, née von Hardenberg.
1794	Meets Madame de Staël in Switzerland (19 September).
1795	Arrival with Madame de Staël in Paris. Divorce from Wilhelmine becomes official.
1797	Birth of Albertine de Staël, probably Constant's daughter.
1799–1802	Member of the Tribunate.
1800–1	Passion for Anna Lindsay.
1804	Trip to Germany with Madame de Staël. Among other visits, a stay in Weimar where Constant meets Goethe and Schiller.
1805	At Julie Talma's deathbed in Paris. Constant alternates between Paris, Coppet, Genève, Lausanne. (These peregrinations are typical of Constant's whole life, and especially of the years up to 1816, but they cannot all be recorded here.)
1806	Passion for Charlotte Dutertre, formerly von Marenholz.

1807	Crisis in Constant's relations with Madame de Staël. 1 September: attempt to escape from Coppet. Interest in Quietism.
1808	Constant secretly marries Charlotte in Besançon.
1809	Charlotte informs Madame de Staël of the marriage. Continued oscillations of Constant. Charlotte's attempted suicide.
1811	Final rupture with Madame de Staël. Constant goes to Germany with Charlotte.
1812	Marital difficulties. Death of Constant's father.
1814	Renewed political activity of Constant. Meetings with Bernadotte. Return to Paris. Interview with Czar Alexander. Sudden passion for Madame Récamier.
1815	Anti-Napoleonic article in the *Journal des Débats*. Member of the imperial Council of State and chief author of the "Additional Act to the Constitutions of the Empire". In Brussels at the end of the year.
1816	With Charlotte in London. Return to Paris.

1817	Death of Madame de Staël in Paris.
1818	Through the Government's intrigues, Constant is beaten in the elections.
1819	Constant elected as deputy for the Sarthe.
1824	Constant elected as deputy for Paris.
1827	Deputy for the Lower Rhine (Alsace).
1830	July revolution. Together with Sébastiani, Constant issues a declaration in favour of the Duke of Orléans. Member of Louis-Philippe's Council of State. 8 December: Constant's death. 12 December: state funeral.

CONSTANT'S PUBLISHED WORKS

There is no complete edition of Constant's works. The best, indeed the only edition of selected works is: Benjamin Constant, *Oeuvres*, Bibliothèque de la Pléiade (Paris, 1957), *texte présenté et annoté par* Alfred Roulin.

The following is a chronological list of first editions. It contains only the most important of Constant's numerous political writings. The place of publication is always Paris, unless otherwise indicated.

De la force du gouvernement actuel et de la nécessité de s'y rallier (1796, or rather "an IV").

Des réactions politiques (1797, "an V").

Des effets de la Terreur (1797, "an V").

Des suites de la contre-révolution de 1660 en Angleterre (1798, "an VI").

Wallstein (Genève et Paris, 1809).

De l'Esprit de conquête et de l'Usurpation dans leurs rapports avec la civilisation européenne (Hanover, 1814; further editions appeared the same year in London and Paris).

Réflexions sur les constitutions, la distribution et les garanties dans une monarchie constitutionnelle (1814).

Principes de politique applicables à tous les Gouvernements représentatifs et particulièrement à la constitution actuelle de la France (1815).

De la responsabilité des ministres (1815).

Adolphe (first appeared in 1816, both in London and Paris).

De la doctrine politique qui peut réunir les partis en France (1816).

Entretien d'un électeur avec lui-même (1818, appeared anonymously).

Collection complète des ouvrages publiés sur le Gouvernement représentatif et la constitution actuelle de la France, formant une espèce de Cours de politique constitutionnelle, 4 volumes (1818–19).

De la liberté des anciens comparée à celle des modernes (1819).

Mémoires sur les Cent-Jours, en forme de lettres (first part 1820, second part 1822).

De la religion considérée dans sa source, ses formes et ses développements (vol. I: 1824; vol. II: 1825; vol. III: 1827; vol. IV and V: 1831).

Discours à la Chambre des députés, 2 volumes (1827–1828).

"Réflexions sur la tragédie", in *Revue de Paris*, VII (1829).

Mélanges de littérature et de politique (1829).

Du polythéisme romain considéré dans ses rapports avec la philosophie grecque et la religion chrétienne, 2 volumes (1833).

Le Siège de Soissons, published by V. Waille (Poligny, 1892).

Journal intime de Benjamin Constant et Lettres à sa famille et à ses amis (1895). This first edition of Constant's Journals, published by D. Melegari, is incomplete and not entirely reliable. The best and most authentic version is that which was first published in 1952, under the title *Journaux intimes*, with an introduction, notes, and an index by Alfred Roulin and Charles Roth. It is this version which is to be found in the Pléiade edition of the *Oeuvres*.

Le Cahier rouge de Benjamin Constant, published by C. Constant de Rebecque (1907).

Les Chevaliers, roman héroïque (1932), published by M. G. Rudler. Written by the twelve-year-old Constant in Brussels in 1779.

Cécile (1951). With introduction and notes by Alfred Roulin.

Large parts of Constant's correspondence have been published. Here I mention only the *Correspondance de Benjamin Constant et d'Anna Lindsay*, published by the Baroness Constant de Rebecque

(1933), and the *Correspondance de Benjamin et de Rosalie de Constant*, published with an introduction and notes by Alfred and Suzanne Roulin (1955).

Constant also wrote the article "Christianisme" for the *Encyclopédie Moderne* and the article "Religion" for the *Encyclopédie Progressive*. The former was published as an extract in 1825 and the latter in 1826.

ENGLISH TRANSLATIONS

There are several English translations of *Adolphe*. The first, by Alexander Walker, was published in London in 1816 (the very year of appearance of the first French edition) and in Philadelphia in 1817. A more recent translation is to be found in J. M. Murry's book *The Conquest of Death* (London and New York, 1951).

A translation of *Adolphe* and *The Red Notebook*, with an introduction by Harold Nicolson, appeared in London in 1948.

A translation of *Cécile*, by N. Cameron, was published in London (1952) and in Norfolk, Conn. (1953).

The *Esprit de conquête* was edited and translated by Helen Byrne Lippmann in *Prophecy from the Past; Benjamin Constant on Conquest and Usurpation* (New York, 1941).

Some political articles by Constant can be found in *The Pamphleteer*, London (1815 and 1821).

SELECT BIBLIOGRAPHY

In English, there are two full-length biographies of Benjamin Constant:

Nicolson, Harold George, *Benjamin Constant* (London, 1949).

Schermerhorn, Elizabeth W., *Benjamin Constant; his private life and his contribution to the cause of liberal government in France, 1767–1830* (Boston & New York, 1924).

Among the critical essays on *Adolphe*, I mention J. M. Murry's book *The Conquest of Death* (London and New York, 1951) and Martin Turnell's excellent chapter on Constant in his book *The Novel in France* (New York).

A good bibliography of the extensive French Constant criticism can be found in the above-mentioned Pléiade edition of Constant's *Oeuvres*.